FRANCESCO GIOIA

Peter

The Apostle who denied Jesus
But loved him most

Libreria Editrice Vaticana

Translation from the Italian
John A. Abruzzese

* *Cover illustration:*
The Miraculous Draught of Fish - Flemish Tapestry
of P. Van Aelst after the design of Raphael
Painting Gallery, Vatican City

* *Back Cover:*
Arms of St. Paul, Cloister of the Patriarchal Basilica
of St. Paul Outside the Walls - Rome

* *Photo:*
Photographic Archives, Vatican Museums

© Copyright 2005
Pontifical Administration
Patriarchal Basilica of St. Paul

ISBN 88-209-6961-0

To His Holiness, Pope John Paul II,
Successor of St. Peter.

St. Peter
Mosaic by G. Cesari
St. Peter's Basilica, Vatican City.

PALESTINE
during the Ministry of Jesus

Presentation

This present booklet is the companion to the volume on St. Paul.[1] Like that work, it is intended for those who come to Rome to venerate the tombs of the Apostles.

Its purpose is also the same: to retrace the spiritual journey of St. Peter and thereby assist the reader in the arduous task of following Christ, who alone – as the Apostle states – gives salvation.[2]

Hearing the preaching of St. Peter at Pentecost, "devout men from every nation under heaven," who came to Jerusalem to celebrate the feast of Passover, "were cut to the heart" and asked: "What shall we do?" St. Peter and the Apostles responded: "Repent" (*metanoésate*)!"[3].

---

[1] Cf. F. Gioia, *Paul of Tarsus: The Apostle for All to Know*, Vatican Press, Vatican City, 2002; *The Apostle Paul: The Testimony of Joy Amidst Suffering*, Vatican Press, Vatican City, 2004; *St. Paul: from "Persecutor and Man of Violence" to "Greatest Model of Patience,"* Vatican Press, Vatican City, 2004; *"We are One Body": The Message of Paul to a Divided World*, Vatican Press, Vatican City, 2004.

[2] Cf. Acts 4:12.

[3] Cf. Acts 2:5, 37-38.

These same words are addressed to us so that we might increasingly realize in our lives, in our constant state as "beggars of heaven,"[4] the same process of conversion as experienced by the Apostle Peter, who denied Jesus but loved him the most.

+ Francesco Gioia, Archbishop
Pontifical Administrator
of the Patriarchal Basilica of St. Paul

Rome, 22 February 2005
Feast of St. Peter's Chair, Apostle

---

[4] J. Maritain, *Carnet de notes*, Desclée de Brouwer, 1965, p. 10.

Introduction

After Christ, the Apostle Peter is the figure who most appears in the pages of the New Testament,[5] always heading the list of those disciples accompanying Jesus, who later were called Apostles.[6] Peter is Andrew's brother and the first to follow Christ.[7]

Without changing the historical nature of the events narrated in the Gospels and in *Acts of the Apostles*, the Church recounted them in a pastoral manner. The leading characters are faithfully set forth in such a way that the reader gradually becomes aware of their assigned mission.

From this perspective, Peter increasingly acquires a more significant place in relation to the other disciples of Jesus.

In *Mark's Gospel*, written probably in 60 A.D. and held to be the oldest of the Gospels (the one from which Matthew and Luke relied), Peter appears clearly as the most important of the Apostles and a model-disciple for his generous yet weak nature.

---

[5] In the four Gospels the name of Peter (with its variants of Cephus, Simon and Simon Peter) occurs 154 times and the name of John appears 120 times. In *Acts of the Apostles* Paul is mentioned 128 times and Peter only 56 times. Among works dealing with the subject of Peter in the Bible is a recently published, scholarly and popular book, entitled *Pietro, roccia della Chiesa* by M. Mazzeo, Daughters of St. Paul, Milan, 2004.

[6] Cf. Mt 10:2-4; Mk 3:16-19; Lk 6:13-16; Acts 1:13.

[7] Cf. Mk 1:16-20; Mt 4:18-22; Lk 5:1-11.

Mark draws attention to Peter's weak nature in various accounts.

The first is that of the Transfiguration of Jesus on Mount Tabor. Peter, unmindful of the meaning of Christ's manifestation, wishes to set up three tents so that the event could last forever. Mark – and Luke after him – makes an excuse for his ingenuous thought, stating that "he did not know what to say."[8]

In Mark and Matthew, Peter, in response to Jesus' unexpected and disconcerting announcement of his Passion, Death and Resurrection, completely overlooks Christ's mention of a resurrection and "reproaches" his Master. Jesus then "reproaches" him – the word appears in Mark only – because he is not thinking according to God but according to men. Jesus even calls him "Satan,"[9] because he is tempting him from submitting to God's will, just like the devil did at the beginning of his ministry.[10]

Though all three Apostles fall asleep in the Garden of Gethsemani, despite Jesus' request that they stay awake to pray with him, Mark draws attention to Peter and the reproof which the Master directs at him only: "Simon, are you asleep? Could you not watch one hour?"[11]

Once again, though all the Apostles fall and abandon the Master in the time of his Passion,[12] all four Evangelists give the account

---

[8]   Mk 9:6; Lk 9:32.
[9]   Cf. Mk 8:33; Mt 16:21-23.
[10] Cf. Mt 4:1-11.
[11] Mk 14:37.
[12] Cf. Mk 14:50.

of Peter's denial.[13] Mark even points out that Peter "invokes a curse on himself and to swear"[14] so as to give more credibility to his affirmation that he did not know Jesus.

The account in Mark – and Luke after him – of the confession at Cesarea Philippi is not as dramatic as that of Matthew. In the former, Peter simply acknowledges Jesus as Messiah, while in the latter he proclaims Christ "Son of the Living God."[15]

In *Matthew's Gospel*, written sometime after 80 A.D. (some 10 years after that of Mark, on which Matthew relies), Peter's weak nature is clearly present everywhere. However, the same Evangelist exclusively narrates three episodes which show Peter's privileged position in relation to the other Apostles.

In the first episode Jesus reproaches the Apostle Peter because he is a "man of little faith;" indeed, Peter fails to recognize Jesus walking on the sea.[16]

The second episode, narrated a little later, has Christ praising Peter for a faith which permits him to see that the Master is not only "Messiah" but also "Son of the living God." In turn, Christ calls him "blessed" by reason of his faith, which is explainable only as a divine gift. Peter then is not simply a "stumbling block;"[17] he is also the firm "rock" on which

---

[13] Cf. Mk 14:66-72; Mt 26:69-75; Lk 22:55-62; Jn 18:17, 25-27.

[14] Mk 14:71.

[15] Cf. Mk 8:29; Mt 16:16; Lk 9:20.

[16] Cf. Mt 14:28-31.

[17] Mt 16:23.

Christ will build the Church and the recipient of the keys of the kingdom of heaven.[18]

In the third episode, the money collectors of the Temple ask Peter why his Master does not pay the temple tax. Jesus calls upon Peter to pay it, for both of them, with the money miraculously to be found in the mouth of a fish.[19] It is worth noting that Matthew emphasizes not only that the tax is paid through Peter but also that whoever wishes to approach Jesus does it through Peter, and not directly as, for example, the disciples of John did, when they asked the Master why his disciples did not fast.[20]

Furthermore, Matthew not only begins the list of the Twelve with the name of Peter, as do Mark and Luke,[21] but he expressly adds the word "first:" "The names of the twelve Apostles are these: first Simon, who is called Peter...."[22]

Only in Matthew does Peter ask Christ, in the name of the others, why his disciples are not bound by Jewish dietary laws.[23] He takes the initiative ("he approached Jesus") of bringing up the subject of forgiveness, a very important matter for the first Christians: "Lord, how often shall my brother sin against me, and I forgive him?"[24]

---

[18] Cf. Mt 16:16-19.
[19] Cf. Mt 17:24-27.
[20] Cf. Mt 9:14.
[21] Cf. Mk 3:16-19; Lk 6:14-16.
[22] Mt 10:2.
[23] Cf. Mt 15:15.
[24] Cf. Mt 18:21.

Luke's Gospel, dating from 80-90 A.D., is generally more favourable towards Peter, giving little account to, or entirely omitting, facts and expressions which might damage his image.

This is clearly seen at the outset in the call of Peter, which occurs in the solemn setting of the miraculous catch of fish, recounted only by Luke,[25] who probably used the story to symbolize the future success of the humble fisherman of Galilee, called to be from that time forward a "fisher of men." Mark and Matthew recount the call of the first disciples in a more sober fashion.[26]

To save Peter's image, Luke omits Jesus' reproof and his calling Peter "Satan," when, in reaction to Jesus' announcement of his Passion, Peter advises Christ to avoid suffering.[27]

Luke also omits mentioning him by name, saying that "one of them" in Gethsemani cut the ear of the slave of the high priest. Moreover, Luke immediately remedies the harm caused by the Apostle's impulsive character by recounting that Jesus touches the ear and heals it.[28]

The only negative aspect appearing in Luke is Peter's denial. Yet even here, the Evangelist seeks to lessen it in some manner by adding a detail which expresses Jesus' goodness and love towards the Apostle: "He turned and looked at Peter."[29]

---

[25] Cf. Lk 5:1-11.
[26] Cf. Mk 1:16-20; Mt 4:18-22.
[27] Cf. Lk 9:22.
[28] Lk 22:50.
[29] Lk 22:61.

Both Luke and John omit Jesus' prediction: "You will all fall away because of me this night."[30] In fact, Luke has Jesus say the contrary: "You are those who have continued with me in my trials;"[31] and records – the only one among the Evangelists – the prayer that Jesus makes for Peter: "Simon, Simon, behold, Satan demanded to have you, that he might sift you like wheat, but I have prayed for you that your faith may not fail; and when you have turned again, strengthen your brethren."[32]

Unlike Matthew who through the images of the "rock" and the "keys" and the action of "binding-loosing" assigned the primacy to Peter in the Church, Luke gives Peter the work of a missionary who must rekindle and strengthen the faith of the brethren, as he will indeed do in *Acts of the Apostles*. This task is similar to the role of "shepherding," given Peter by John.[33]

Finally, Luke intimates that Jesus has forgiven Peter through his unique retelling of the account of the disciples on the road to Emmaus, specifying that the Risen Christ appeared to Simon only.[34]

The Gospels of Matthew and Luke provide a portrait of Peter at the end of the first century, similar, for the most part, to that of Mark about 20 years earlier.

---

[30] Mt 26:31; Mk 14:27.
[31] Lk 22:28.
[32] Lk 22:31-32.
[33] Cf. Jn 21:17-21.
[34] Cf. Lk 24:34.

In *John's Gospel*, written about 90-95 A.D., Peter has prominence more than any other disciple, including "the disciple Jesus loved."

John alone illustrates Peter impulsive character in recounting the episode at the Last Supper in which he refuses to have Jesus wash his feet. In the end, however, he begs the Master not only to wash his feet but also his hands and head.[35]

His impulsiveness is also seen in the account of the miraculous draught of fish. In addition to taking the initiative to go fishing and drag the net of fish ashore, he instinctively "jumps into the sea" to go and meet Jesus, after having discovered that the unknown person on shore was the Risen Lord.[36]

Only John identifies Peter as the disciple who struck the slave of the high priest.[37] However, the Evangelist measures his words in Peter's regard, by having Jesus appeal to him no longer to use the sword and simply to recall for Peter that he must "drink the cup which the Father has given him."[38]

Jesus' words indicate that Peter still did not embrace the idea that the Master had to suffer, despite that fact that Christ clearly said it after Peter's confession at Cesarea Philippi. Where the accounts of Matthew and Mark have Christ calling Peter "Satan," in John's Gospel, Jesus does not reproach Peter for this refusal to accept a suffering Messiah.

---

[35] Cf. Jn 13:6-11.
[36] Cf. Jn 21:1-14.
[37] Cf. Jn 18:10.
[38] Jn 18:10-11.

John also does not mention the reproof found in Matthew after Peter wounds the slave of the high priest. He simply records the following admonition: "Put your sword back into its place; for all who take the sword will perish by the sword. Do you think that I cannot appeal to my Father, and he will at once send me more than twelve legions of angels? But how then should the scriptures be fulfilled, that it must be so?"[39]

Only in John's Gospel does Jesus offer Peter the possibility of redeeming himself for having denied him three times. Christ asks Peter three times if he loves him more than the others; and following each question, Christ commands Peter to tend his sheep.[40]

Since Peter is to be like the Good Shepherd who lays down his life for the sheep,[41] Jesus predicts his death using a metaphor which seems to allude to his martyrdom in Rome. He calls on Peter to follow him in this regard and then reproaches him for inquiring about the lot of the beloved disciple.[42]

In some instances John seems indifferent when he speaking of Peter. Indeed, the account of Peter's confession ("You are the holy one of God"[43]) is less dramatic than that of Matthew: ("You are the Christ, the Son of the living God"). Furthermore, in John's Gospel, Jesus does not praise Simon, as he does in Matthew,

---

[39] Mt 26:52-54.
[40] Cf. Jn 21:15-17.
[41] Cf. Jn 10:11.
[42] Cf. Jn 21:18-22.
[43] Jn 6:69.

when Peter proclaims him to be "Son of the living God:" "Blessed are you, Simon Bar-Jona! For flesh and blood has not revealed this to you, but my Father who is in heaven."[44]

Peter, who has asked Jesus to have allow him to follow him,[45] is not present at the foot of the cross; there are only Mary, his mother, and the "disciple he loved," who is entrusted with Mary.[46]

John's Passion and Resurrection accounts have an unnamed disciple,[47] oftentimes described as "the disciple whom Jesus loved"[48] or simply as "the other disciple."[49] This disciple is said to enjoy a special intimacy with the Mas-

---

[44] Mt 16:17.

[45] Cf. Jn 13: 36-37.

[46] Cf. Jn 19:26-27.

[47] The redactor of Chapter 21 of *John's Gospel* attributes the Fourth Gospel to this unnamed disciple (cf. 21:24). It is unknown whether he is an authentic historical character, or simply a theological figure or symbol of the ideal disciple. This is not surprising, if one considers the spiritual and theological character of John's Gospel, as Clement of Alexandria observes: "John, the last of the Gospel writers, having seen that material events were already set forth by the other Gospels, was encouraged by his disciples and divinely inspired by the Spirit to compose a Gospel spiritual in nature." (Eusebius, *Historia Ecclesiastica*, 6, 14, 7). Christian tradition has identified the unnamed disciple as the Apostle John, but his true identity remains unknown. Some scholars venture beyond tradition and attempt to identify him in the following manner: 1) an historic disciple of Jesus who did not belong to the Twelve; 2) the founder and spokesman of a Joannine school of thought and author of the Fourth Gospel; 3) a symbolic figure who personifies the ideal disciple; and 4) a purely literary character.

[48] Cf. Jn 13:23; 19:26-27; 21: 7, 20, 23-24.

[49] Cf. Jn 18:15-16; 19:26-27; 20:2-4, 8.

ter, as demonstrated by the fact that at the Last Supper, he "lies close to the chest of Jesus."[50]

He is the only disciple who does not flee during Jesus' Passion, thereby making him the lone exception to Jesus' prediction: "The hour is coming, indeed it has come, when you will be scattered, every man to his home, and will leave me alone."[51] As a result he is seen to personify the ideal disciple of Christ.

Three biblical scenes associate the beloved disciple and Peter: the Last Supper;[52] the courtyard of the high priest[53] and Easter morning, when the disciple reaches the Jesus' tomb before Peter and finds it empty. In this last scene the beloved disciple is said to "see and believe."[54] Together they are witnesses of the central event in their Master's life.

They understand each other well and, judging from certain details, it can be argued that they even shared basic ideas.

In *Acts of the Apostles*, written about 80-85 A.D., Peter is a prominent figure in the spread of Christianity as narrated in the first 15 chapters, with the exception of the chapters 9 and 13 which are dedicated to Paul. The Apostle Paul is the principal character in the remaining thirteen chapters. After chapter 15, Peter is no

---

[50] Jn 13:25.
[51] Jn 16:32.
[52] Cf. Jn 13:23-26.
[53] Cf. Jn 18:15-16.
[54] Cf. Jn 20:2-10. Only in this episode "the beloved disciple" is identified with "the other disicple" (thus designated four times).

longer mentioned. In many ways, Luke often parallels the activity of the two Apostles.

In his Gospel, Luke places Peter last in the list of the Twelve, while in *Acts of the Apostles*, he is the first to be named, probably to affirm that the Twelve, sent into the whole world to continue their Master's work,[55] serve as the bridge between the historical Christ and the Church in the world.[56]

In this mission Peter has a uniquely special role, documented in the fact that he is the first to announce the Resurrection of Christ to not only the Jews[57] but also the Gentiles.[58]

His missionary activity exhibits a courage which characterized the preaching of the prophets.[59] On four occasions, he publicly attributed the responsibility for Jesus' death to the Jews[60] and his boldness (*parresía*) stunned the Sanhedrin.[61] They forbade John and him to speak of Jesus, but they responded: "Whether it is right in the sight of God to listen to you rather than to God, you must judge; for we cannot but speak of what we have seen and heard."[62]

---

[55] Cf. Mt 28:19-20; Mk 16:15, 16, 15-16; Lk 24:47-48.
[56] This role of the Twelve is also highlighted by the fact that the Synoptic Gospels (Matthew, Mark and Luke) close with the mandate to proclaim the Gospel to all creation and that *Acts of the Apostles* opens with the same command: "You shall be my witnesses...in all of Judea and Samaria to the end of the earth" (1:8).
[57] Cf. Acts 2:14-36.
[58] Cf. Acts 11:34-43.
[59] Cf. F. Gioia, *Il coraggio di sperare contro ogni speranza*, Cinisello Balsamo, San Paolo 2001.
[60] Cf. Acts 2:23, 36; 3:14; 10:40.
[61] Cf. Acts 4:13.
[62] Acts 4:19-20.

On various occasions, God miraculously intervened to free him from prison[63] and guide him in the work of bringing the Gospel to the Gentiles.[64]

In *Acts of the Apostles*, Peter is also portrayed as a great miracle worker,[65] so much so that the sick are cured with the mere passing of his shadow.[66]

Luke highlights the important role played by Peter in the election of a successor to Judas[67] and during the "Council of Jerusalem," which probably took place in 49 A.D..[68]

The figure of Peter is also present in *Paul's Letters*.

Writing around 54-55 A.D. to the community at Corinth, where Peter was held in high

---

[63] Cf. Acts 5:17-21; 12:6-11. Paul is also miraculously set free from prison (cf. Acts 16:25-34).

[64] Cf. Acts 10:9-16. On various occasions, divine intervention is at work in Paul life, not only at his conversion (cf. Acts 9:3-7; 22:6-11; 26:13-18), but also in reaching Macedonia (cf. Acts 16:9) and continuing his mission in Corinth (cf. Acts 18:9-10), Rome (cf. Acts 23:11) and other circumstances (cf. Acts 20:22-23; 21:10-11; 27:23-24).

[65] Peter heals a lame man (cf. Acts 3:1-10) and a paralytic (cf. Acts 9:32-35) and raises a woman to life (cf. Acts 9:36-42). Paul also cures a paralyzed man (cf. Acts 14:8-18) and raises a boy from the dead (cf. Acts 20:7-12). There are similarities among the miracles of the two Apostles and those of Jesus. For Peter, compare Acts 9:40 with Mk 5:41; for Paul, Acts 28:7-10 with Mk 1:30-31.

[66] Cf. Acts 5:15. Luke similarly writes concerning Paul: "And God did extraordinary miracles by the hands of Paul, so that handkerchiefs or aprons were carried away from his body to the sick, and diseases left them and the evil spirits came out of them" (Acts 19:11-12).

[67] Cf. Acts 1:15, 26.

[68] Cf. Acts 15:5-11.

esteem by many Christians,[69] Paul places Cephas at the head of the list of persons to whom the Risen Christ appeared.[70]

Paul acknowledges Peter's authority. In fact, after three years from his conversion, in about 37-38 A.D., he goes to Jerusalem to "consult Cephas" and remains there fifteen days[71] to avoid the risk of "running in vain"[72] in his work as Apostle. He insists that he is fully aware that "he who worked through Peter for the mission to the circumcised worked through him also for the Gentiles."[73]

Paul relates in the Letter to the Galatians, written about 55-56 A.D., how at Antioch Peter and Paul discussed the proper way to treat Christian converts from paganism. Without scruple, Peter eats food with pagan converts; but after the arrival of the Judaizers (Jewish converts to Christianity) he starts to avoid them for fear of being criticized. From Paul's perspective, such behaviour seemed hypocritical. He therefore "opposed him (Peter) to his face, because he stood condemned," and reproached him: "If you, though a Jew, live like a Gentile and not like a Jew, how can you compel the Gentiles to live like Jews?"[74]

It is worth noting that Paul opposes Peter not as head of the apostolic college but as an

---

[69] Cf. 1 Cor 1:12; 3:22. In the same letter, reference is made to Cephas and his wife who is accompanying him (cf. 9:5).
[70] Cf. 1 Cor 15:5.
[71] Cf. Gal 1:18-19.
[72] Gal 2:2.
[73] Gal 2: 8.
[74] Gal 2:11-14.

individual who acted against the fundamental principle of freedom given by Jesus Christ.

The episode illustrates that the relationship between the two Apostles was characterized by frankness and openness. In the end, at the "Council of Jerusalem," where the matter was discussed anew, James, Cephas and John, "reputed to be pillars" of the Christian community, gave to Paul and his co-worker Barnabas "the right hand of fellowship as a sign of communion."[75]

Addressing Christians of every age, Luke states that the Gospels were written to increase faith: "that you may know the truth concerning the things of which you have been informed."[76] All things considered, "all scripture is inspired by God and profitable for teaching, for reproof, for correction, and for training in righteousness, that the man of God may be complete, equipped for every good work."[77]

The Evangelists' theological vision, their intent and the Christian communities to which they write, determine what events they decide to include or omit and how they portray various personages.

Based on the various references found in the New Testament texts and the latest biblical exegesis, Peter is portrayed as going beyond the various associations resulting from his actions and becomes an ordinary disciple both in his passionate love for Jesus and the weak nature of his faith.

---

[75] Gal 2:9.

[76] Lk 1:4.

[77] 2 Tm 3:16.

St. Peter Seated in his Chair
Giotto di Bondone
Painting Gallery, Vatican City.

St. Peter
P. Lorenzetti
Painting Gallery, Vatican City.

1. "Woe to you Bethsaida! And you, Capernaum, will you be exalted to heaven? You shall be brought down to Hades!" [78]

Bethsaida, Aramaic for "the home of fishermen," is situated on Lake Tiberias; it was "the city of Andrew and Peter."[79] Jesus worked two miracles in this city: the multiplication of the loaves, as recounted by Mark and Luke,[80] and the healing of a blind man.[81]

Peter probably lived a great part of his life in Capernaum, given that he had a house and family there.[82]

Capernaum, one of the most important cities in Galilee, was located on the western coast of Lake Tiberias, near the place where the Jordan flows into the Lake. Because the *Via Maris*, joining Mesopotamia to the Mediterranean, passed through the town, Capernaum was a crossroads of sorts. It was also a significant cultural center with a synagogue and nationally renowned rabbinical schools.[83] There were also customs houses[84] and a praesidium of the

---

[78] Mt 11:21-23; Lk 10:13-15.
[79] Jn 1:44.
[80] Cf. Mk 6:45; Lk 9:10.
[81] Cf. Mk 2:22.
[82] Luke notes that Jesus, leaving the synagogue in Capernaum, "entered the house of Simon," where he cured his mother-in-law (cf. 4:38-39; cf. Mt 8:14-15; Mk 1:29-31).
[83] Cf. Mk 1:21; Lk 4:31-33; Jn 6:59.
[84] Cf. Mt 9:9.

Roman guard.[85] The city was divided in two: the higher part was reserved for offices and the upper class, and the lower part for workers and people of more modest means.

The cosmopolitan environment, with its commercial and cultural exchange, certainly had an effect on Peter's character. His contemporaries, James and John, were called "sons of thunder"[86] by Jesus, because of their fiery temperaments. Peter's character would not have been much different. Despite all possible attenuations, the Gospels portray him as an open-minded man, spontaneous, decisive and often impulsive.

He is a common fisherman, used to hard and oftentimes disappointing work, as he himself reminds Jesus: "Master, we have toiled all night and have caught nothing."[87] Jesus chooses Peter's boat as a pulpit to teach the crowds.[88] His brother Andrew is also a fisherman;[89] both are co-workers with James and John, sons of Zebedee,[90] in what can be called a "cooperative venture." In any case, Peter's social status was not very high, yet he did not occupy the lowest rung of the social ladder.

Jesus lived in Capernaum for a time.[91] He left the heights of Nazareth and came to this region which was more suited to his work of preaching. Indeed, Capernaum was the site of many

---

[85] Cf. Mt 8:5-13.
[86] Cf. Mk 3:17.
[87] Lk 5:4; cf. Jn 21:3-4.
[88] Cf. Lk 5:3.
[89] Cf. Mt 4:18; Mk 1:16.
[90] Cf. Lk 5:10.
[91] Cf. Mt 4:13; Jn 2:12.

of Jesus' discourses and the place in which he worked miracles.

In Capernaum, Jesus gave, among others, the discourse on the "bread of life;"[92] he called Levi or Matthew to follow him;[93] he healed a demoniac and many who were ill; he cured Peter's mother-in-law,[94] a paralytic,[95] the slave of the centurion,[96] and the woman with a hemorrhage on the way to raising the daughter of Jairus from the dead;[97] according to Matthew, he also cured two blind men and a dumb demoniac.[98]

However, despite the miracles Jesus worked in Bethsaida and Capernaum, the inhabitants remained incredulous and, consequently, were strongly upbraided by Jesus: ""Woe to you, Chorazin! woe to you, Bethsaida! for if the mighty works done in you had been done in Tyre and Sidon, they would have repented long ago in sackcloth and ashes. But I tell you, it shall be more tolerable on the day of judgment for Tyre and Sidon than for you. And you, Capernaum, will you be exalted to heaven? You shall be brought down to Hades. For if the mighty works done in you had been done in Sodom, it would have remained until this

---

[92] Cf. Jn 6:59-66.
[93] Cf. Mk 2:14; Mt 9:9; Lk 5:27-28.
[94] Cf. Mt 8:14-16; Mk 1:21-34; Lk 4:31-41.
[95] Cf. Mk 2:1-12; Mt 9:1-8.
[96] Cf. Mt 8:5-13; Lk 7:1-10. For John the Evangelist, this cure was "the second miracle which Jesus did, returning from Judea in Galilee" (4:54).
[97] Cf. Mt 9:18-26; Mk 5:21-43; Lk 8:40-56.
[98] Cf. Mt 9:27-33.

day. But I tell you that it shall be more tolerable on the day of judgment for the land of Sodom than for you."[99]

Bethsaida and Capernaum were not pagan cities like Tyre and Sidon on the Phoenician coast; nor did the people live the morally perverted lives which caused the destruction of Sodom. Nevertheless, no conversions were made among the inhabitants, despite the fact that, in the region, Jesus preached and performed – according to Matthew – "most of his mighty works."

Matthew recounts that at Capernaum the local tax collectors asked Peter if Jesus had paid the taxes for the upkeep of the Temple at Jerusalem. Every male Jew over twenty years of age was required to pay this tax annually.[100]

The Apostle Peter responds in the affirmative. However, after arriving at the home of Jesus to inform him about what had happened, the Master tells a short parable: "What do you think, Simon? From whom do kings of the earth take toll or tribute? From their sons or from others?" Peter responded: "*From others.*" And Jesus concludes: "Then the sons are free. However, not to give offense to them, go to the sea and cast a hook, and take the first fish that comes up, and when you open its mouth you will find a shekel; take that and give it to them for me and for yourself."[101] Jesus' thought is clear: his followers, who share a common

---

[99] Mt 11:20-24; cf. Lk 10:13-16.
[100] Cf. Ex 30:11-16; Neh 10:33.
[101] Mt 17:24-27.

Father[102] and whom he considers sisters and brothers,[103] are absolved from paying such a tax; nevertheless, according to the law of love, they are obliged not to give scandal and, consequently, they pay it.

This episode is strongly symbolic. The Evangelist wishes to highlight the pre-eminence of Peter in relation to the other Apostles and the necessity of his mediation by recounting that the tax collectors do not approach Jesus directly, but through Peter, who shortly before was chosen as the "rock" on which Jesus will build his Church.

At Capernaum, as Jesus prays in a lonely place after a long day of healing, Simon and the others go in search of him and say: "*Everyone is searching for you!*", because "they wanted him to stay," as Luke notes. But Jesus responds: "Let us go on to the next towns, that I may preach there also; for that is why I came. And the same Evangelist states that "and he was preaching in the synagogues of Judea and casting out demons." [104]

---

[102] Cf. Mt 5:45.
[103] Cf. Mt 12:50.
[104] Cf. Mk 1:35-38; Lk 4:42-44.

The Call of St. Peter and St. Andrew
Fresco by D. Ghirlandaio
Sistine Chapel, Vatican City.

St. Peter
Fra Bartolomeo
Apostolic Palace, Vatican City.

2. "Do not be afraid, henceforth, you will be fishers of men!" [105]

From that fateful day in which Jesus of Nazareth encountered Peter on the shore of the lake, his life changes radically. The Gospels do not chronicle all that took place nor do they relate how everything happened. Perhaps the meeting was not the first encounter he had with Jesus, who caused the people to marvel at his teaching, "because he taught as one with authority and not like the Scribes," [106] and who elicited praise because of his mighty works: "All marveled and praised God, saying: 'We never saw anything like this,'" according to Mark, after Jesus healed the paralytic. [107]

Jesus' meeting with Simon and his brother Andrew seems to be fortuitous. It happens, according to Matthew and Mark, "while he (Jesus) walked along the Sea of Galilee," [108] namely, Lake Gennesaret, [109] also called Tiberias. [110] The same two Evangelists state that Jesus "saw." It is not simply a matter of sight but a prophetic look allowing Jesus to perceive in these men a possible response to a call which would make them participants in his mission.

---

[105] Lk 5:10.
[106] Mk 1:22; cf. Mt 7:28; Lk 4:32.
[107] Mk 2:12; Mt 9:8; Lk 5:26.
[108] Mt 4:18; cf. Mk 1:16. John, instead, refers to the banks of the Jordan River and the community of John the Baptist (cf. 1:35-42).
[109] Cf. Lk 5:1.
[110] Cf. Jn 6:1.

When the Evangelists narrate the call of the first disciples many years after the event, the account becomes the blueprint for every vocation, that is, Jesus' choice ("he saw"), the decisive call ("follow me") and the wholehearted response of those called ("immediately they followed him").

Luke[111] is less dramatic in recounting the event and is perhaps more faithful in describing the actual situation in which the first followers were called.

There is a crowd which "near the lake" gathers around Jesus to hear "the word of God." Nearby are some fishermen who are washing their nets. To avoid the press of the crowd and the risk of being pushed into the sea, Jesus gets into Peter's boat which is among others close by. He then asks to be pushed out a little from the shore. From this special pulpit he continued his conversation with the people.

From the choice of Simon's boat one can presume a certain familiarity between the two of them. This also explains the trustful tone of voice in the words which Simon addressed to Jesus when he tells him to cast out into the deep and let down his nets for a catch: *"Master,*

---

[111] Cf. Lk 5:1-11. Matthew and Mark omit the episode of the miraculous catch of fish. In a certain way, a parallel can be found in John in the account of the apparition of the Risen Lord on the shore of Lake Tiberias. (cf. 21:1-14). The two accounts have the following similarities: the central figure is always Simon Peter; the disciples have fished all night without success; Jesus orders them to lower their nets; the fish are so abundant as to create difficulty with the nets; the Apostle is called Simon and Jesus is addressed with the title "Lord;" among the other fishermen who are silently present at the catch are the sons of Zebedee; and after the catch, Jesus calls them to follow him.

we have toiled all night and took nothing! But at your word I will let down the nets."

Jesus' command was clearly folly to Simon and his companions who were seasoned fishermen. Indeed, fishing in daylight would be futile and would not lead to a great catch of fish.

Simon's trust in Jesus, expressed in his calling him "Master," was rewarded in a great shoal of fish. The miracle caused "astonishment" in all present. Simon himself, clearly acknowledges, on the one hand, the mysterious power of the one who gave the order to lower the nets in full daylight. He now calls Jesus "Lord," and no longer "Master," as he had first done. On the other hand, he becomes aware of his lowly human condition: *"Depart from me for I am a sinful man, O Lord."* One can imagine that Peter made the profession of his unworthiness "on his knees" and with a tone of voice which reveals his loss of words in witnessing the miraculous catch.

Jesus' response is totally unexpected: "Do not be afraid; henceforth you will be catching men."

Jesus offers Peter another kind of work which is seen to parallel, in certain way, what he has been already doing. He will always remain a "fisherman," but a "fisher of men." He will be called to another kind of sea, i.e., history, the environment where people live their everyday lives.

His brother, Andrew, and his companions, James and John, fishermen like him,[112] will also be "fishers of men."[113] However, in Luke, Jesus gives this title to Simon alone, probably

---

[112] Mark notes that "they were fishermen" (1:16).
[113] In Mark (1:17) and Matthew (4:19) Jesus says to both Peter and his brother Andrew: "Follow me, I will make you become fishers of men."

because of the prominent role he will have among the Twelve in *Acts of the Apostles.*

"Fishers of men" might seem a little gratifying, almost ambiguous, expression, since it gives the impression that people can be caught dishonestly by fraud, as a net surprises and entraps the fish. However, the expression is taken from the trade they exercise, and involves, in some way, the work which they must do, even if with profoundly different means at hand: people are not caught but are attracted and seized by the Gospel.

According to Matthew, fishing-with-a-net symbolizes the Kingdom of Heaven: the net is lowered into the sea and gathers every kind of fish, which is subsequently divided into the good and bad.[114]

If Simon's efforts brought him nothing and the fish entered the net solely by Jesus' intervention, it is clear that Peter, the Fisherman of Galilee, will have success as a "fisher of men," because of God's power, despite the fact that he is a sinner.

In every way, this kind of "fishing" is more arduous than that to which they are presently accustomed. It is difficult for fish to escape the net, but people can run from the net; they can destroy it and even do harm to those who lower the net. In the metaphor "fishers of men," Jesus does not fully explain everything, but he clearly offers an idea that the mission of the Apostles will always be an uneasy endeavour,

---

[114] Cf. Mt 13:47-50. The other three Evangelists omit this parable, which in its theological meaning, is very similar to that of the weeds, recounted solely by Matthew (cf. Mt 13:24-30, 36-43).

difficult and toilsome, because it involves the free choice of those called to conversion.

Simon, his brother Andrew,[115] the two "companions," "James and John, sons of Zebedee," and the other Apostles[116] responded immediately to the Lord's call. Some might say that it was not sufficiently pondered by them, but no one can say that it was not a courageous act for

---

[115] Unlike Matthew and Mark, Luke does not mention the calling of Andrew, brother of Peter.

[116] The fifth disciple, to which Jesus says: "Follow me," is the publican Levi. He receives his call while at his tax office. His response is also immediate: "And he rose and followed him," abandoning a very profitable, if hated, profession as tax collector (cf. Mk 2:14; cf. Mt 9:9).
John the Evangelist recounts the call of the sixth and seventh Apostle. Jesus encounters Philip and says to him: "Follow me!" The readiness and the enthusiasm with which the new disciple accepts the call is seen in the words addressed to his friend Nathanael, called Bartholomew in the list of the Twelve in the Synoptic Gospels (cf. Mt 10:2-3; Mk 3:16-19; Lk 6:13-16; Acts 1:13): "We have found him of whom Moses in the law and also the prophets wrote, Jesus of Nazareth, son of Joseph" (Jn 1:45). Nathaniel expresses his perplexity at the humble origin of the Messiah: "Can anything good come out of Nazareth?" (Jn 1:46). However, Philip's faith looks beyond the appearances of a carpenter's son and says to his friend: "Come and see" (Jn 1:46). Natanael "approaches Jesus" (Jn 1:47) who expresses his esteem for him and reveals that he has already known him for some time: "Behold an Israelite indeed, in whom there is no guile. Before Philip called you, when you were under the fig tree, I saw you" (Jn 1:47:48). He is awe-struck by the Master's words and acknowledges him to be the Messiah: "Rabbi, you are the Son of God, you are the King of Israel" (Jn 1: 43-51).
We know nothing about the call of the other five Apostles (James, son of Alphaeus, Simon the Canannite or Zealot, Thaddeus or Jude, son of James, Thomas and Judas Iscariot); the biblical texts record only the names of the first three; while Thomas and Judas appear in various biblical accounts.

them to leave their nets and their families: "And when they brought their boats to land, they left everything and followed him (*ekoloúthesan*)."[117]

The verb *akolouth eín* does not mean simply to move from one place to another in following someone; it has a theological meaning: some common fishermnen follow him in a spiritual sense, that is, they become his close collaborators.

The call of Peter, Andrew and the other two brothers develops and grows in this climate of familiarity and enthusiasm.

For Luke, the miracle of the fish explains why the Apostles leave all to follow Jesus. Their response to the Master's call comes after due spiritual preparation, namely – in the sequence of Luke's Gospel – after listening to his preaching and witnessing various miracles, like the cure of Peter's mother-in-law.[118]

The accounts of the Apostles' call have a certain plan to them; they are more a "model" than an "historic event." Nevertheless, a basic truth remains, namely, the capacity of these men to give themselves wholeheartedly to an unknown person simply at his word and to believe in a preacher who until then had not clearly set forth the plan he had in mind.

From what follows in the biblical accounts, it could perhaps be said that the fishermen of Galilee entertained some romantic illusions about Jesus. He might have appeared in their eyes as a political guide or someone who would restore Israel's destiny. However, he gave no

---

[117] Lk 5:11. Matthew (4:22) and Mark (1:18, 20) add that "immediately" they left their nets and point out that, in addition to the boat, they also left their "father."

[118] Cf. Lk 4:38-39.

indication that he was either. A little later, these "men of little faith,"[119] will ask Jesus, who will be the greatest in the Kingdom of Heaven.[120] They will even squabble among themselves for the first places in the group[121] and, right up until the drama of Golgotha, they have thoughts of the return of the old Davidic kingdom.[122] Whatever the case, these aspirations reveal the Apostles to be men of great courage, because they have placed their hopes in a person who has not indicated that he can achieve any of these things.

Over a period of time in the company of Jesus, Peter, a practical man, *speaks* on behalf of the other Apostles and asks what they will receive in return for their generosity to Jesus: "*Lo, we have left everything and followed you. What then shall we have?*".

Jesus reassures them, saying that the reward will be infinitely superior to what they have given up: "And every one who has left houses or brothers or sisters or father or mother or children or lands, for my name's sake, will receive a hundredfold, and inherit eternal life."[123] Mark points out that recompense is received also at "the present time," possibly an allusion to what took place in the first Christian community, which was characterized by a great fraternal love and the total sharing of goods.[124]

When Luke writes, the apostolic call has already become an apostolic mission: The

---

[119] Mt 8:26; cf. 14:31; 16:8.
[120] Cf. Mt 18:1-4.
[121] Cf. Mt 20:20-23; Mk 10:35-40.
[122] Cf. Acts 1: 6, 27-29.
[123] Cf. Mt 19:27-29; cf. Mk 10:28-31; Lk 18:28-30.
[124] Cf. Acts 4:32; 2:44.

early Christian community was like a new ship which embarked on a sea wider than the Lake of Galilee. Its course is sure, however, because, in the absence of Christ, Peter guides it.

Matthew and Mark call Simon "Cephas," (Peter) in their Gospels.[125] John, instead, has Jesus call Peter by this name: "Jesus looked at him and said: 'So you are Simon the son of John? You shall be called Cephas' (which means Peter)."[126]

From this time onwards, the Gospels use these names in designating Simon; they eventually become the name under which he is commonly known. The Greek word *Pétros* and the corresponding word in Aramaic *KephBs* were not used as a person's name before Jesus used them in reference to Simon.

The change of name already shows that Peter is to play an important role in the community of Jesus' followers. In the Bible, a change of name has always had a prophetic meaning, indicating a special mission entrusted by God to leading characters in salvation history, as for example, Abraham,[127] Sarah,[128] Jacob[129] and Gideon.[130]

In being given the name "Peter," Simon is to perform an action of sustaining or supporting the apostolic community, details of which are given in the Synoptic Gospels. Peter will not be a stone that crumbles, but a rock which is firm and steadfast.

---

[125] Mt 10:2; Mk 3:16.
[126] Jn 1:42. In John's Gospel, Jesus never uses the name "Peter," but always that of "Simon."
[127] Cf. Jn 17:5.
[128] Cf. Jn 17:15.
[129] Cf. Jn 32:29.
[130] Cf. Jdgs 6:7.

3. "Then Peter came up and said to him..." [131]

Simon Peter is always prominent in the group of those most faithful to Jesus; oftentimes he acts as their *spokesman*.

After the discourse on fraternal correction,[132] Peter asks Jesus: "*Lord, how often should my brother sin against me, and I forgive him?*" The Apostles words manifest the generosity of his heart, given that the number 7 for the Semites indicated fullness, completeness and perfection. Jesus responds: "I do not say to you seven times, but seventy times seven."[133]

The expression "seventy times seven" is not intended in a mathematical sense; instead the expression means that forgiveness must be limitless.

Jesus illustrates his teaching with the parable of the merciless servant, whose lord cancelled his enormous debt. He encounters a fellow servant who owes him a paltry sum and not being able to repay him, he has him thrown into prison. Learning of this, the lord then "delivered him (the merciless servant) to the jailers, till he should pay all his debt," namely, he condemned him to life imprisonment, given that he would never be able to pay such an exorbitant sum. The moral of the parable is that forgiveness of one's neighbour is the condition for God's forgiving our sins. "So also my heavenly Father will do to every one of you,

---

[131] Mt 18:21.
[132] Cf. Mt 18:15-18; Lk 17:3.
[133] Mt 18:21-22; cf. Lk 17:34.

if you do not forgive your brother from your heart."[134]

Jesus had already taught recourse to prayer for the grace to forgive others with the same generosity with which God forgives our sins: "And forgive us our debts, as we also have forgiven our debtors."[135]

In Mark's Gospel, as Jesus prays in a lonely place, after spending the entire day curing people, Simon and others from Capernaum find Jesus. Speaking for the group, he says: "*Everyone is searching for you!*" The expression shows that, after witnessing the miracles performed by Jesus, the people desire that he stay with them. Jesus responds to Peter with words indicating his decisiveness to continue his travels: "Let us go on to the next towns, that I may preach there also; for that is why I came out!"[136]

After Jesus' somewhat enigmatic discourse or "parable" on legal impurity and moral purity,[137] Matthew says that Peter asked: "*Explain the parable to us.*" The Master has just set forth the general principle: "What goes into the mouth does not make a man impure, but what comes out of his mouth." The disciples, however, did not understand; so Jesus specifies: "Are you still without understanding? Do you not see that whatever goes into the mouth passes into the stomach, and so passes on? But whatever comes out of the mouth proceeds from

---

[134] Cf. Mt 18:23-35.
[135] Mt 6:12.
[136] Cf. Mk 1:35-38. In Luke a crowd goes in search of Jesus (cf. 4:42-44). Mathew makes no mention of the episode.

42

the heart, and this defiles a man. For out of the heart come evil thoughts, murder, adultery, fornication, theft, false witness, slander. These are what defile a man; but to eat with unwashed hands does not defile a man." Jesus cites only one example of the numerous prescriptions concerning legal impurity, namely, the Pharisees teach that to eat without washing one's hands ("purifying oneself") defiles the food.

After Jesus recounts the parables of the master who unexpectedly returns from a wedding and of the thief who comes without notice, Luke states that in both cases Peter is the one to ask: "*Lord are you telling this parable for us or for all?*"[138] Jesus responds with another parable: that of the "faithful and wise steward, whom his master, arriving unexpectedly, will find working."[139]

In the episode of the woman with the hemorrhage, when Jesus asks who touched him, "all denied it." Again Peter is the one to interject: "*Master, the multitudes surround you and press upon you!*"[140]

On the following day when Jesus cursed the fig tree which had an abundance of leaves but totally lacking any fruit – a symbol of the con-

---

[137] Cf. Mt 15:10-20; Mk 7:14-23. Mark omits Peter's name and says only that the disciples asked for the explanation of the "parable" (cf. 7:17). Luke makes no mention of this "parable."

[138] Lk 12:41.

[139] Cf. Lk 12:42-48; Mt 24:45-51.

[140] Lk 8:45. In Mark, Peter's observation is made by the disciples (cf. 5:31).

demnation of Judaism which hides its lack of good works under a leafy display of religious formalism – it is again Peter who points out to the Master that the plant was withered: *"Master, look! The fig tree that you cursed is withered."*[141]

Peter was most likely the spokesman for James, John and Andrew,[142] who were also present, when Jesus announced the destruction of the Temple in Jerusalem.[143] He asks the Master two questions "in private:" *"Tell us, when will this be, and what will be the sign when these things are all to be accomplished?"*

Jesus' response to the first question is: "But of that day or that hour no one knows, not even the angels in heaven, nor the Son, but only the Father."

For this reason, Jesus will insist that vigilance is needed: "Take heed, watch and pray; for you do not know when the time will come."[144] Some parables also teach this lesson: the master who departs without announcing the precise time of his return, and, as a result, the servants are advised to be ready at any moment to welcome him;[145] the thief who comes without

---

[141] Mk 11:21. In Matthew (21:20) the "disciples" ask for the explanation why the fig tree withered immediately after the Master's curse.

[142] They are the first four disciples whom Jesus called to be Apostles (cf. Mk 1:14-20).

[143] Cf. Mk 13:1-32. Matthew (cf. 24:1-3) and Luke (cf. 21:5-7) do not mention the names of the disciples who pose the question to Jesus.

[144] Mk 13:33; cf. Mt 24:36, 42; 25:13.

[145] Cf. Mk 13:34-37; Mt 25:45-51; Lk 12:35-48.

warning;[146] and the ten virgins who await the bridegroom without knowing the exact time of his arrival.[147]

Jesus responds to the second question posed by the three Apostles with a long eschatological discourse in which he announces the trials in store for the disciples, the tribulation of Jerusalem and cataclysmic cosmic events.[148]

---

[146] Cf. Mt 24:43; Lk 12:39.
[147] Cf. Mt 25:1-12.
[148] Cf. Mk 13:5-31; Mt 24:4-31; Lk 21:8-33.

Christ Entrusts the Keys to St. Peter
Perugino
Sistine Chapel, Vatican City.

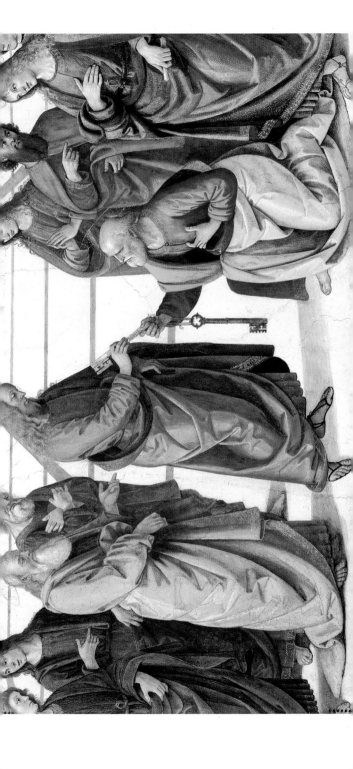

St. Peter and Pope Eugenius IV
Filarete
Bronze Doors of St. Peter's Basilica, Vatican City.

4. "You are the Christ, Son of the living God!"[149]

When in the region of Cesarea Philippi, Jesus wanted to know what people thought of him.[150] His disciples said that some, like those at the court of Herod Antipas[151] thought he was John the Baptist returned from the dead; others said he was Elijah, the prophet who, according to popular belief, was to announce the end of time;[152] still others held that he was Jeremiah, who tradition stated would return to restore the ark and the sacred objects hidden from the moment of the exile;[153] there were also those who simply thought Jesus to be one of the prophets.[154]

The disciples made no mention of the other opinions. Indeed, there were those who identified him as the Messiah;[155] who held him to be a "Good Teacher,"[156] "the Saviour of the World"[157] and "Son of David."[158] In responding to the Lord's question, the Apostles failed to tell him that "there was division among the people over him,"[159] and that some of

---

[149] Mt. 16:16.
[150] Cf. Mt 16:13-20; Mk 8:27-30; Lk 9:18-21.
[151] Cf. Mt 14:2; Lk 9:7; Mk 6:13.
[152] Cf. Mt 17:10.
[153] Cf. 2 Micah 2:1-12; 15:13-16.
[154] Cf. Jn 4:19; Lk 24:19; Jn 1:41; 4:29.
[155] Cf. Mt 12:23; Jn 6:14.
[156] Mk 10:17; Lk 18:18.
[157] Jn 4:42.
[158] Cf. Mt 9:27; 15:22; 20:30; 21: 9, 15.
[159] Jn 7:43; cf. 10:19-20.

his enemies maintained he was "possessed,"[160] "mad,"[161] an "impostor,"[162] a "troublemaker,"[163] a "glutton and drunkard,"[164] a "Samaritan,"[165] a "blasphemer,"[166] and a "friend of sinners."[167]

But when he directs the question to the Apostles: "But you, who do you say that I am?", Peter is the one to speak for the group and acknowledges not only his Messiahship but also his divine origin: *You are the Christ, the Son of the living God.*[168]

In response, Jesus indicates that the source of Peter's knowledge is not the result of human research or reckoning, but the exclusive fruit of a divine revelation personally communicated to Peter: "Blessed are you, Simon Bar-Jona! For flesh and blood has not revealed this to you, but my Father who is in heaven."

---

[160] Jn 10:20; 7:20; 8:48, 52; Mt 12:24; Mk 3:22.

[161] Jn 10:20; Mk 3:21.

[162] Mt 27:63.

[163] Lk 23:2.

[164] Lk 7:34.

[165] Jn 8:48. The Samaritans were considered an "impure" race resulting from intermarriage between the Israelites, who remained in that area after the Assyrian exile (721 B.C.), and people coming from other parts of the East (cf. 2 Kings 17:24-41).

[166] Cf. Jn 10:33; Mt 9:3; 26:55; Mk 2:6; Lk 5:21.

[167] Cf. Lk 7:34; 15:2.

[168] Mark and Luke record only Peter's declaration concerning the Messiahship of Jesus: "You are the Christ" (Mk 8:29; Lk 9:20) and omit the expression "Son of the living God." Jesus' divine nature is also acknowledged by John the Baptist (cf. Jn 1:34), the possessed man in the land of the Gerasenes (cf. Lk 8:28) and the Roman centurion after Christ's Death (cf. Mt 27:54). In his encounter with the Risen Christ, the Apostle Thomas exclaims: "My Lord and my God" (Jn 20:28).

Peter is the only disciple to be designated as "blessed", that is, "enjoying particular favour," a prerogative which gives him a special place among Jesus' disciples.

In this episode, he is not voicing a tenet of a faith held in common with the other Apostles. His acknowledgment comes from a personal faith which is a God-given gift.

After this proclamation of Jesus' Messiahship comes Christ's solemn declaration, recounted only in Matthew: "And I tell you: 'You are Peter and on this rock (*epì taúte tê pêtra* = *kephà*) I will build (*oikodoméso*) my Church, (*moù tèn ekklesíam*) and the powers of death shall not prevail against it. I will give you the keys of the kingdom of heaven, and whatever you bind on earth shall be bound in heaven, and whatever you loose on earth shall be loosed in heaven'."[169]

This text is the basis for "Peter's primacy" in the fullest sense of the term. The Lord's declaration is the basis for all of Peter's powers. Christ's words leave no manner of doubt, as seen in age-old and present biblical exegesis.

Simon's full power in his mission as prime shepherd of the Church is illustrated in three metaphors.

The first is the *rock* (*pétra-kephà* or *Pétros-kephàs*) on which rises the foundation (the Church) that death and evil cannot destroy, just as, in the parable, the wise man's house-built-on-rock is sheltered from the tempest.[170]

---

[169] Mt 16:16-19.
[170] Cf. Mt 7:24-25.

The Church is not a material structure; but – according to another metaphor – it is the community constructed of "living stones," which must find their cohesion by remaining attached to the cornerstone.[171]

The second image is the *keys* which, by their nature, are already indicative of power. In the Bible this meaning is clearly expressed in the case of Eliakìm, head of the household of Hezekiah, who received the keys of the kingdom of David as a sign of the powers which he must exercise in the king's absence.[172]

The third image is the dual concepts of *binding-loosing*, which allude to the spiritual and doctrinal responsibilities of Peter. In the rabbinic schools the expression "binding and loosing" was used "to declare" a determined interpretation of the law as "true or false," or to retain some manner of acting as "licit or illicit." The connotation of the word "to loose" is "to free" or "to permit," while "to bind" means "to impede."

Matthew notes that "from that time," namely, after Peter's confession, Jesus begins to speak openly and no longer through parables about his Passion, Death and Resurrection. When Peter first hears this unexpected announcement, he shows his intemperate zeal: "He took him and began to reproach him, saying: *'God forbid, Lord, this shall never happen to you'*."

Peter, in his person, displayed the great shock of the Apostles; they did not understand

---

[171] Cf. 1 Pt 2:4-5.
[172] Cf. Is 22:20-22; cf. 2 Kings 18:18.

the mission of their Master who had to suffer much so as to "enter into his glory,"[173] as Jesus recalled for the disciples of Emmaus. But, "they understood none of these things,"[174] because they were awaiting a Messiah-King, who would restore the kingdom of Israel in which the brothers, James and John, directly asked Jesus for the privileged places at his side.[175]

Jesus response to Peter is a harsh one: "Get behind me, Satan! You are a hindrance to me; for you are not on the side of God, but of men." [176]

Peter, allowing himself to be guided only by human reason, placed himself in opposition to God's designs and became "a hindrance" (*skándalon*); hence he is called "Satan."

---

[173] Cf. Lk 24: 26.
[174] Lk 18:34; cf. Mk 9:45.
[175] Cf. Mk 10:35-40. Matthew, to somewhat lessen the ambitious character of the two brothers, has their mother make the request (cf. 20:20-23).
[176] Mt 16:21-23; Mk 8:31-33.

5. "Lord, to whom shall we go?
You have the words of eternal life!
And we have believed
and have come to know
That you are the Holy One of God"[177]

Peter voices the reaction of the Twelve after the Jesus' Eucharistic discourse in the synagogue at Capernaum,[178] exclusively recounted by John the Evangelist, who puts it immediately after the multiplication of the loaves.

The crowd, which was present for the miracle of the loaves,[179] asks Jesus for another miraculous "sign," similar to that of the manna, which Moses had done to feed the Jews during their long sojourn in the desert.[180] In this way, Jesus would reveal himself and be accredited as someone sent by God.

On the subject of the manna, Jesus qualifies: "It was not Moses who gave you the bread from heaven; my Father gives you the true bread from heaven. For the bread of God is that which comes down from heaven, and gives life to the world."

Jesus' listeners, taking his words literally, understand this extraordinary bread to be a kind of food which totally alleviates hunger; and so they beg: "Lord, give us this bread always!"

---

[177] Jn 6:68-69.
[178] Cf. Jn 6:22-69.
[179] Cf. Jn 6:1-13; Mt 14:13-21; Mk 6:32-44; Lk 9:10-17.
[180] Cf. Ex 16:1-35; Ps 78:24.

A similar misunderstanding takes place with the Samaritan woman. When Jesus said to her: "Whoever drinks of the water that I shall give him will never thirst," she promptly responds: "Sir, give me this water, that I may not thirst."[181]

The misunderstanding of those who heard Jesus declaration leads him to state explicitly: "I am the bread of life; he who comes to me shall not hunger, and he who believes in me shall never thirst."[182]

This statement causes a clamor among the Jews, who begin to "murmur" at his words: "Is not this Jesus, son of Joseph, whose father and mother we know? How does he now say, 'I have come down from heaven?'."[183]

Jesus further insists: "I am the bread of life. Your fathers ate the manna in the wilderness,

---

[181] Jn 4:15. Neither does Nicodemus understand Jesus' words: "Unless one is born anew, he cannot see the kingdom of God." This is evident in his question: "How can a man be born when he is old? Can he enter a second time into his mother's womb and be born?" (Jn 3:4).

[182] Jn 6:34, 48-51. "I am the Bread of Life" is one of many expressions called *egó eimí* ("I am"), which reveal Jesus' divinity and occur frequently in John's Gospel: "I am the bread come down from heaven" (6:35, 41, 48, 51); "I am the light of the world" (8:12; 9:5); "I am the sheep gate" (10:7, 9); "I am the Good Shepherd" (10:11, 14); "I am the Resurrection and the Life" (11:25); "I am the Way, the Truth and the Life" (14:6); "I am the True Vine" (15:25). Indirect references to "living water" (4:10, 14; 7:37) can be added to these expressions as well as the general use of "I am" (8:24, 28, 58; 13:19) which recalls the great revelation of God's name to Moses (cf. Ex 3:14). "I am" is also found in Isaiah (cf. 43:10) and Ezechial (cf. 6:7, 10, 13, 14).

[183] Likewise in the account of the manna, the Jews "murmur" against Moses (cf. Ex 16:2, 7-8). This serves to illustrate, albeit implicitly, that the Evangelist sees a parallel between the manna and the multiplication of the loaves.

and they died. This is the bread which comes down from heaven, that a man may eat of it and not die, I am the living bread which comes down from heaven.; if anyone eats this bread, he will live for ever; and the bread which I shall give for the life of the world is my flesh."

Hearing these latest statements, which are even more daring than the preceding ones, the Jews "began to dispute among themselves."

Jesus develops his thought still further: "Unless you eat of the flesh of the Son of man and drink his blood, you have no life in you; he who eats my flesh and drinks my blood has eternal life, and I will raise him up at the last day."

Those in the crowd are not the only ones disturbed by the Master's words; the disciples too are "scandalized" and say: "This is a hard saying, who can listen to it?" "There were some (among them) who did not believe." Consequently, the Evangelists records that "many of his disciples drew back and no longer went about with him."

The Gospel records the Master's reaction to the departure of so many disciples; he wants to hear the opinion of the Twelve: "Will you also go away?" They must openly declare whether they will stay with him or leave him.

Again speaking for the Twelve, Simon Peter solemnly declares: *"Lord, to whom shall we go? You have the words of eternal life; and we have believed, and have come to know that you are the Holy One of God."* [184]

---

[184] The words in John closely resembles those uttered by Peter in the Synoptic accounts of the confession at Cesarea Philippi: "You are the Christ, Son of the living God." (Mt 16:16; cf. Mk 8:29; Lk 9:20).

For Peter, Jesus' words are not "hard," because he does not simply "say" the words of eternal life, but he "has" those words in his possession. John contrasts the disbelief of "some disciples" with the Apostles' faith, which acknowledges in their Master "the Holy One of God," namely, one sent by God and one who has a unique relationship with God, continually noted by the Evangelist: "the Father has sanctified him and send him into the world."[185]

Peter will also apply the title of "Holy" to Jesus not only in his discourse to the people after healing the cripple but also in the prayer during his trial before the Sanhedrin.[186]

---

[185] Jn 17:18-19.

[186] Cf. Acts 3:14; 4:27, 30. In the Synoptics, the Messianic title, "Holy One of God," comes forth from the mouth of demons (cf. Mk 1:24; Lk 4:34).

6. "Lord, it is well that we are here!"[187]

Peter also *speaks* on behalf of the Apostles at the Transfiguration.[188] According to Matthew and Mark, the event happens six days after Peter's profession in Christ's divinity; Luke has it take place "about eight days" later.

Jesus took Peter, James and John[189] and led "them up a high mountain apart. And he was transfigured before them, and his face shone like the sun, and his garments became white as light."[190]

Two important personages from the Old Testament appeared next to the transfigured Christ: Moses and Elijah, who represent the Law and the Prophets respectively. Their presence confirms for the three Apostles that Jesus came to fulfill the law and not destroy it and to complete all that was predicted by the prophets.[191] Jesus himself stated as much to confute

---

[187] Mt 17:4.

[188] Cf. Mt 17:1-8; Mk 9:2-8; Lk 9:28-36; 2 Pt 1:16-18.

[189] These three Apostles, who witnessed his transfiguration, are the only ones allowed to be present, apart from the parents, when Jesus raises Jairus from the dead. Mark and Luke draw attention to the amazement of these five people and the prohibition of Jesus to tell no one (cf. Mk 5:37; Lk 8:51). In Matthew's account, no one witnesses the miracle (9:25).
According to Mark and Matthew, Jesus also chooses Peter, James and John to accompany him to the Garden of Gethsemani to watch and pray with him (cf. Mk 14:32-38; Mt 26:36-41).

[190] Mark describes the event in a simple picturesque style: "And his garments became glistening, intensely white, as no fuller on earth could bleach them" (9:3).

[191] Cf. Lk 4:21; Acts 3:22-24.

the accusations of the Scribes and Pharisees: "Think not that I have come to abolish the law and the prophets; I have come not to abolish them but to fulfill them."[192]

Before this scene Peter "says to Jesus: '*Lord, it is well that we are here; if you wish, I will make three booths here, one for you and one for Moses and one for Elijah*'".

Peter's proposal is generous yet naive, typical of his straightforward and impetuous character. It does not occur to him that these special people have no need of booths. Above all, he fails to understand that the nature of the event is only a glimpse of Jesus' glory, meant to confirm for the three disciples the divine identity of their Master, who is Son of God and destined to suffer, die and rise again from the dead.

Mark, and Luke after him, excuses Peter for his words, saying that "he did not know what to say." James and John now enter the picture, as the two Evangelists tell what gave rise to Peter's words. Mark states: "because they were exceedingly afraid;" and Luke: "because they were heavy with sleep."

As on the day of Christ's Baptism,[193] a voice from heaven reveals Jesus' true identity: "This is my beloved son, listen to him."

Matthew alone states that, in viewing this great theophany, the three Apostles "fell on their faces, and were filled with awe." Jesus then touched them and reassured them: "Have no fear!" Coming to their senses, they "saw no

---

[192] Mt 5:17.
[193] Cf. Mt 3:17; Mk 1:11; Lk 3:22.

one except Jesus," who by then had returned to how they normally saw him.

Luke is the only Evangelist who associates the transfiguration with Jesus' death, noting that Moses and Elijah "spoke of his departure, which he was to accomplish at Jerusalem." Luke's message is quite clear: the Messiah who now appears in splendour will in a short time meet a humiliating and painful end.[194]

The miracle of the transfiguration made such an impression on Peter that he recalls it in the second letter which bears his name: "We were eyewitnesses of his majesty. For when he received honour and glory from God the Father and the voice was borne to him by majestic glory, 'This is my beloved Son, with whom I am well pleased,' we heard this voice borne from heaven, for we were with him on the holy mountain."[195]

---

[194] Matthew and Mark mention Jesus' death in the conversation on Elijah's return, which Jesus has with the three Apostles as they come down the mountain.

[195] 2 Pt 1:16-18.

7. "Man of little faith, why did you doubt?" [196]

At the sight of Jesus coming to them on Lake Tiberias, the disciples are terrified, thinking he is a ghost. The Master reassures them: "Take heart, it is I, have no fear!"

In recounting this episode, the intention of Mark, Matthew and John[197] is not simply to highlight the miracle; nor is it to emphasize that the Master is close to his disciples, though they be unaware, as "the boat is beaten by the waves for the wind was against them." Their purpose is to focus on the manifestation of Christ: Christ, radiant from afar in the darkness of the night, stands for the Risen Christ.

Peter, doubting the Master's real identity asks: "*Lord, if it is you, bid me to come to you on the water.*"

Jesus grants his wish: "Come!" The Apostle begins to walk on the water, but "when he saw the wind, he was afraid and began to sink." His faith remains even before this danger, because with faith in his Master, he cries out: "*Lord, save me.*" The Master took him by the hand and saved him. However, he reproaches him: "Man of little faith (*oligópistos*), why did you doubt?"

Scarcely after Jesus and Peter got into the boat, the wind ceased and "those in the boat

---

[196] Mt 14:31.
[197] Cf. Mt 14:22-27; Mk 6:45-52; Jn 6:16-21. Luke omits this episode.

worshiped him, saying, 'Truly you are the Son of God!'"[198]

It is highly symbolic that Peter, the "rock" on which the Church is to be built, sinks! Matthew is interested in demonstrating that Jesus saved Peter at the very moment he begins to sink and calls for help.

Mark closes the event with Jesus getting into the boat, the wind ceasing and the disciples remaining "utterly astounded, for they did not understand about the loaves, but their hearts were hardened."[199]

The request to walk on water reveals Peter's desire, like other biblical characters in the past, to have a proof of the goodness and omnipotence of his Master.

Moses asks God for signs to prove the legitimacy of his mission to the People of Israel. God then transformed his shepherd staff into a serpent; and he healed his hand after it became leprous.[200]

Gideon, sent by God to conquer the Midianites, asked: "If I find favour in your sight, give me a sign that it is really you who is speaking to me."[201]

Zaccariah, at the announcement of the birth of John the Baptist, asks: "How shall I know this? I am an old man and my wife is advanced in years."[202]

Similarly, Mary asks the Angel Gabriel: "How can this be, since I have no husband?" And the

---

[198] Cf. Mt 14:28-33. Matthew is the only Evangelist to narrate this episode.
[199] Mk 6:52.
[200] Cf. Ex 4:1-9.
[201] Cf. Jdg 6:16-17.
[202] Lk 1:18.

Angel said: "And behold, your kinswoman Elizabeth in her old age has also conceived a son; and this is the sixth month with her who was called barren. For with God, nothing will be impossible."[203]

The Pharisees and Sadducees demand that Jesus "show them a sign from heaven."[204] And the crowd, called upon by Jesus to believe in him after the multiplication of the loaves, asks: "Then what sign do you do, that we may see, and believe in you?"[205].

In the analogous episode found in the Synoptics,[206] the disciples find themselves in an unexpected, violent storm. They wake the Master and shout: "Save us, Lord, we are perishing!" Jesus admonishes them, using the same words he addressed to Peter: "Why are you afraid, men of little faith?" He then calms the lake, causing "a great fear" in them, that is, they are astonished at Jesus' power over the forces of nature.

When the Apostles discover that they are weak in faith, they say to the Lord: "Increase our faith." Jesus then responds: "If you had faith as a grain of mustard seed, you could say to this sycamine tree, 'Be rooted up, and be planted in the sea,' and it would obey you."[207] From this we learn that the power of faith defies even the laws of nature, because a plant is unable to live in sea water.

---

[203] Lk 1:36-37.
[204] Mt 12:38.
[205] Jn 6:30.
[206] Cf. Mt 8:23-27; Mk 4:35-41; 11:22; Lk 8:22-25.
[207] Lk 17:5-6. Matthew (17:20; 21:21) and Mark (11:23) report only the exhortation of Jesus to have faith and omit the request of the Apostles.

St. Peter Seated in his Chair
Bronze statue attributed to Arnolfo di Cambio
St. Peter's Basilica, Vatican City.

The Denial of St. Peter
Attributed to Pensionante del Saraceni
Painting Gallery, Vatican City.

8. "Though they all fall away because of you, I will not fall away! Even if I must die with you, I will not deny you!" [208]

Only Luke records that Jesus gave Peter and John the task of preparing for the Passover feast. They said to him: *"Where will you have us prepare?"* and Jesus gave them precise indications what they were to do. [209]

During the washing of the feet – recounted only in John's Gospel – Jesus explained the meaning of this act: "If I then, your Lord and Master, have washed your feet, you also ought to wash one another's feet. For I have given you an example, that you also should do as I have done for you."

But when it was Peter's turn, Simon Peter said. *"Lord, do you wash my feet?"* Jesus replied: "What I am doing you do not know now, but afterward you will understand." Peter objects: *"You shall never wash my feet!"* Jesus emphasizes the necessity of it: "If I do not wash you, you have no part of me." Yielding to the Master's wish, Peter shows his impulsive temperament: *"Lord, not my feet only, but also my hands and my head."* [210]

John also highlights Peter's impulsive character, when Jesus is arrested in the Garden of

[208] Mt 26:33, 35; Mk 22:29, 31. Peter's affirmation is not as forceful in Luke as in Matthew and Mark: "Lord, I am ready to go with you to prison and to death" (22:33).

[209] Cf. Lk 22:8-13.

[210] Cf. Jn 13:1-20.

Gethsemani. "Simon Peter, who had a sword," in attempting to keep his Master from arrest "pulls it out and strikes the slave of the high priest, cutting off his right ear." At this Jesus reproaches him: "Put your sword into its sheathe." At the same time, he tells him, as he did on various occasions,[211] that his passion and death are part of the Father's Will[212] which he must accept.

After the institution of the Eucharist, the Synoptics record a long conversation between the Master and the Apostles.

Matthew and Mark refer to Jesus prophecy: "You will all fall away because of me this night; for it is written, 'I will strike the shepherd, and the sheep of the flock will be scattered.' But after I am raised up, I will go before you to Galilee."

Peter said: *"Though they all fall away because of you, I will never fall away."* Jesus replies: "Truly I say to you, this very night before the cock crow, you will deny me three times." Peter then says: *"Even if I must die with you, I will not deny you."* Mark adds that Peter insisted "vehemently."[213]

Luke and John omit the prediction that all the disciples will fall away. In fact, Luke says just the opposite: "You are those who have continued with me in my trials,"[214] and reports the prayer that Jesus says for Peter: "Simon,

---

[211] Cf. Jn 14: 31; Mt 26:39; Mk 14:36; Lk 22:42.
[212] Jn 18:10-11. Matthew (26:51-52), Mark (14:47) and Luke (22:50-51) omit Peter's name.
[213] Mt 26:31-35; cf. Mk 14:26- 31.
[214] Lk 22:28.

Simon, behold, Satan demanded to have you, that he might sift you like wheat, but I have prayed for you that your faith may not fail; and when you have turned again (*epistrépsas*), strenghten (*stérison*) your brethren."[215]

There is an incongruence in the passage between "Simon" and "you (pl.)": Jesus addresses Simon individually but his prayer is for all the Apostles. Most Likely, the reference to Satan's attempt to sift the Apostles like a grain of wheat could be equivalent to the prediction found in Matthew and Mark: "You will all fall away because of me this night."

Perhaps, the power of Jesus' prayer made Peter follow the Master after his arrest, despite the prediction: "You will all fall away; for it is written: 'I will strike the shepherd, and the sheep will be scattered'."[216]

Just as Peter's faith at Cesarea Philippi, with which he acknowledged Jesus as the "Son of the living God," is a gift from the Father,[217] so in this instance, Peter's faith will not grow less. He is to strengthen his brothers, because of the assistance he receives from Jesus' prayer. In both cases, a good outcome does not depend on Peter's strength alone, but on divine assistance.

In John's Gospel, the prediction of Peter's denial comes at the end of the farewell discourse at the Last Supper. Jesus says to the

---

[215] Lk 22:31-32. In the New Testament the term "brethren" indicates "believers;" for example, when John writes: "The saying spread aborad among the brethren..." (Jn 21:23), he intends to say "in the Church."

[216] Mk 14:27; Mt 26:32.

[217] Cf. Mt 16:16-17.

Apostles: "Little children, yet a little while I am with you. You will seek me, but ... where I am going you cannot come." Peter took the Master's words literally and asked him: "*Lord, where are you going?*" Jesus says in response: "Where I am going you cannot follow me now; but you shall follow afterward."

The Apostle, thinking that Jesus is to embark on a dangerous journey or that he doubts his resolve to follow Jesus wherever he will go, reacts in his usual instinctive manner: "*Lord, why cannot I follow you now? I will lay down my life for you!*" Jesus calms Peter's enthusiasm and asks him to reflect on his fragile human nature: "...the cock will not crow, till you have denied me three times."[218]

The Master then announces the betrayal by one of his Apostles without mentioning his name. Deeply disheartened, the Apostles ask one by one if he is the one. Only John mentions Peter and the beloved disciple who asks Jesus to point out his betrayer: "One of his disciples, whom Jesus loved, was lying close to the chest of Jesus; Simon Peter beckoned to him and said, 'Tell us who it is of whom he speaks.'" And John, "lying thus close to the chest of Jesus," asked who it was. The Master says in reply: "It is he to whom I shall give this morsel when I have dipped it." The Evangelist narrates that "when he dipped the morsel, he gave it to Judas Iscariot."[219]

Matthew says, instead, that it was Judas himself to ask Jesus: "Is it I, Master?" Jesus then

---

[218] Cf. Jn 13:33, 36-38.
[219] Jn 13:23-26.

declares openly: "You have said so."[220] Indeed, Judas, after agreeing with the chief priests[221] on the sum of thirty pieces of silver, betrays him with a kiss.[222]

After the meal, Jesus chooses Peter, together with James and John, to accompany him to Gethsemani and pray. Despite this sign of predilection, they fall asleep and do not take part in his "sadness and distress." Jesus admonishes only Peter, however: "Simon, are you asleep? Could you not watch one hour?" Then, turning to the others, he adds: "Watch and pray that you not enter into temptation; the spirit indeed is willing, but the flesh is weak."[223]

[220] Mt 26:26, 25.
[221] Cf. Mt 26:14-16; Mk 14:10-11; Lk 22:3-5.
[222] Cf. Mt 26:48-50; Mk 14:44-45; Lk 22:47-48. John omits Judas' kiss; he says only that he led the soldiers to the place where Jesus was, so they could arrest him (cf. 18:3).
[223] Cf. Mk 14:33-38; Mt 26:36-41.

9. "He began to invoke a curse upon himself and to swear: I do not know this man of whom you speak!" [224]

Though all four Evangelists give an account of Peter's denial, each relates it in a different manner, including certain details which highlight the grave fault of the Apostle yet, at the same time, take into consideration Peter's unique position in the Church.[225]

According to Matthew, when Jesus was arrested and led before the high priest and the Sanhedrin, Peter followed him at a distance and entered into the courtyard of the palace.[226] He was then recognized as a disciple of Jesus by a few persons.[227]

---

[224] Mk 14:71.

[225] Cf. Mt 26:69-75; Mk 14:66-72; Lk 22:55-62; Jn 18:17, 25-27.

[226] The Synoptics say only that Peter "followed Jesus at a distance" (cf. Mt 26:58; Mk 14:54; Lk 22:54). John states that Simon Peter followed him with "another disciple," whose name remains unknown. This "disciple" knew the high priest and thus is able to enter the courtyard, while Peter remains outside. Peter later enters, after the unnamed disciple speaks with the gatekeeper (cf. 18:15-16).

[227] In Mark's Gospel, Peter is recognized twice by the same maid, who first looks at him ("she fixed her eyes on him") and then perhaps, following him with her eyes, recognizes him among those who were warming themselves by the fire ("having seen him"); the third time Peter is recognized by persons who were in the palace.

In Luke, Peter is first questioned by a maid and a second and third time by two anonymous men.

In John, Peter is questioned the first time by the young gatekeeper, who at the request of the unnamed disciple obtained permission for Peter to enter the palace of the

The first to recognize him was a maid, who asked him: "You were also with Jesus the Galilean!" Peter grows upset and, seeing himself at a loss, responds in an evasive manner, pretending that he does not under-

---

high priest. The second time, the Apostle is questioned by servants and guards who were standing with him warming themselves by the fire. From the way the question is formulated, the first and second time ("Are you not also one of this man's disciples?"), one can legitimately conclude that the accusers are simply suspicious of Peter, based on various impressions. Perhaps they recognize that he is a foreigner from his Galilean accent or from his uncertain, cautious behaviour. The third accuser is one of the servants of the high priests, who was "related to the slave whose ear Peter had cut off" and who had seen him in Gethsemani together with the Master. In this instance, undeniable proof is provided, namely, an eyewitness who was present at Jesus' arrest in Gethsemani and who is accusing him of being not simply Jesus' disciple, but the one who cut off the ear of a Temple guard in the line of duty.

In the Synoptics, those who question Peter state that he "was with Jesus" or that he was "one of them" (one of Jesus' disciples), but without substantiating their claims. The only proof could be that his accent clearly indicated that he came from Galilee, thus making him a countryman and friend of Jesus.

John refers only to the response made by Peter the first and second time he was asked if he were Jesus' disciple: "*No, I am not.*" Such a response is not a true and proper denial, but a lie which already reveals a loss in character. In the other two cases, the Evangelist states only that he denies the Master, without reporting his exact words.

John and Luke omit Peter's swearing and the cursing as recorded in Matthew and Mark, as a sign of respect and esteem for Peter.

The Evangelists clearly distinguish three denials, but, in comparing their respective accounts, there could have been at least five.

The first denial in Mark and Luke happens in the courtyard as Peter is warming himself by the fire; in John, Peter, in similar circumstances, denies Jesus for the second time. Matthew totally omits this detail.

stand the question: "*I do not know what you mean.*"

Both Matthew and Mark state that after the first denial, Peter leaves and goes into the outer portico to mix with the people so as to avoid being recognized again. This particular detail is open to interpretation. It could be said to be a cowardly act. At the same time, however, it could manifest Peter's desire not to be put in a position to deny his Master a second time.

But here, despite his precautions, he finds himself again in the midst of other accusers. Another servant recognizes him and asks the same question, to which he directly and explicity "denies it again with an oath: '*I do not know the man*'."

When those present insist: "Certainly you are also one of them, for your accent betrays you!", the Apostle "began to invoke a curse on himself and to swear: '*I do not know the man!*'."

The gradual increase in the tone of Peter's denial is noteworthy: the first time he makes a simple statement; the second time his denial is accompanied by various oaths; and the third time, it is reinforced by repeated cursing.

All four Evangelist state that the cock crowed.[228] According to the version set forth by Matthew and Luke, Peter recalls the prediction of his denial at cock crow, made by the Master at the Last Supper. Luke adds a particular detail rich in meaning: after Peter denies Christ a third time, "the Lord turned and looked at

---

[228] Mt 26:74; Mk 14:72; Lk 22:60; Jn 18:27. Mark is the only Evangelist to note that the "cock crowed a second time."

Peter. And Peter remembered the word of the Lord, how he said to him, 'Before the cock crows today, you will deny me three times'."[229] Christ's glance makes Peter recall Christ's tragic prediction. It is not only a kind of reproof but also a sign of Jesus' love for Peter.

Stung to the heart as he again pondered Jesus' fateful words, the Apostle Peter immediately left the house of the high priest to avoid denying him still another time. When he was alone, he took into account his grave sin and, as only the Synoptics record, "he wept bitterly."

---

[229] Lk 22:61.

An Angel Frees St. Peter from Prison
Detail, Raphael
Rooms of Raphael, Vatican City.

An Angel Frees St. Peter from Prison
Detail, Raphael
Rooms of Raphael, Vatican City.

10. "Lord, you know everything; You know that I love you!"[230]

In John's Gospel, Peter has a prominent place in the Resurrection accounts. All four Evangelists[231] record that Mary Magdala was the first person to see that the tomb in which Jesus had been buried was empty. Only John says that she went at once to "Simon Peter and the other disciple, the one Jesus loved" to inform them.[232] Peter and John then go to the Lord's tomb.

"The other disciple outran Peter and reached the tomb first; and stooping to look in, he saw the linen cloths lying there, but he did not go in;" he waits for Peter to arrive. Peter then entered first and, after him, the other disciple.[233]

The unnamed disciple does not immediately enter the tomb, because he recognizes a certain authority in Peter. John states that when "the other disciple entered, he saw and believed:" He was not the first to enter, but he was the first to believe. Though it is impossible to give a precise reason for John's including this information,

---

[230] Jn 21:17.
[231] Cf. Mt 28:1, 6; Mk 16:5; Lk 24:3; Jn 20:1-2.
[232] In Matthew (cf. 28:7-8) and Luke (cf. 24:9-10) the women inform the Apostles and other disciples; while in Mark, the Angel tells the women to announce Jesus' Resurrection "to his disciples and to Peter" (16:7), though they said nothing to anyone, because they were afraid (cf. 16:8). The explicit mention of Peter indicates his importance in the apostolic college.
[233] Luke also adds that Peter, even though he and the other Apostles maintain that the announcement of Mary Magdala and the other women to be "an idle tale," "rose and ran to the tomb; stooping down and looking in, he saw the linen cloths by themselves" (24:11-12).

it does not rule out that Peter could also have immediately believed in Jesus' Resurrection.

The Risen Christ appears many times to his disciples.[234] Mark,[235] Luke[236] and Paul[237] expressly refer to Peter in these apparitions as a special witness. John alone gives three accounts of the apparition of the Risen Christ on the shore of Lake Tiberias in which Peter is indisputably the leading figure.[238]

In the first scene, Simon, accompanied by six other Apostles, decides to go fishing. His decision is shared by his companions. They fished for the entire night – the best time for fishing – but "that night they caught nothing."

"Just as day was breaking, Jesus stood on the beach: yet the disciples did not know that it was Jesus. Jesus said to them, 'Children, have you any fish?' They answered him, 'No.' He said to them, 'Cast the net on the right side of the boat, and you will find some'."

The Apostles obeyed this mysterious person and, as the result, "they were not able to haul it (the net) in, for the quantity of fish."

The first one to recognize Christ was "the disciple whom Jesus loved." He therefore said

---

[234] Cf. Jn 20:14, 15-19, 26; 21:4, 13; Mt 28:16-17; Mk 16:9, 12, 14; Lk 24:15, 36; 1 Cor 15:5-8; Acts 1: 3; 10:40-41; 13:31.

[235] The Angel tells the women who went to the Jesus' tomb: "You are looking for Jesus of Nazareth whom they crucified. He is risen; he is not here. Look at the place where they laid him. Now go, tell his disciples and Peter that he goes before them into Galilee. You will see him there, just as he told you" (Mk 16:6-7).

[236] The disciples of Emmaus, after recognizing the Risen Christ, return to Jerusalem and go to see "the Eleven and the others who were with them. They said: 'the Lord is truly risen and has appeared to Simon" (Lk 24: 33-34).

[237] Cf. 1 Cor 15:5.

[238] Cf. Jn 21:1-23.

to Peter: "It is the Lord!" Peter again shows his impetuous character: "When Simon Peter heard that it was the Lord, he put on his clothes, for he was stripped for work, and sprang into the sea." The other Apostles, less instinctively, start to drag the net towards the shore.

When Jesus said: "Bring some of the fish that you have just caught," Simon Peter takes the initiative: "So Simon Peter went aboard and hauled the net ashore, full of large fish, a hundred and fifty-three of them."

The first scene ends with Jesus offering bread and fish to the Apostles to eat.[239]

The second scene opens with the Jesus' question to Peter: "Simon, son of John, do you love me more than these?", namely, more than the other Apostles present. In reply, with no reference to the others, he humbly replies: "*Yes, Lord, you know that I love you.*" In a surprising gesture, Jesus then entrusts to him the supreme authority of the flock, that is, his Church: "Tend my sheep."

Jesus poses the same question to him a second and third time, but without the words, "more than these." The Apostle replies a second time using the same words. However, when asked a third time, Peter "is grieved," probably because he remembered the three times he denied Jesus or perhaps because he thought Jesus doubted his love. So, in his third reply he makes a reference to Christ's omniscience: "*Lord, you know every-thing; you know that I love you.*" Jesus entrusts his sheep to him a second and third time.

---

[239] Unlike Luke's account of the last apparition to the Apostles (cf. 24:41-43), John does not have Jesus eat with his Apostles.

In asking Peter the same question three times, the Master wishes to make his disciple remember, on the one hand, that, on the night before his Passion, Peter had told him that he would not abandon him, even if the others did so,[240] and, on the other hand, he offers him the possibility of redeeming himself, both in his own eyes and in the eyes of the others.

Before Jesus entrusts the flock to Peter, he asks if Peter loves him more than the others so that he could implicitly teach that the love of the one who exercises supreme authority over the flock must exceed all others.

No precise meaning is attached to the verb "to tend." Nevertheless, in some metaphorical sense, it describes Simon's responsibility for the entire flock of Christ, especially if one bears in mind that in the Old Testament the king is designated as "shepherd."[241]

Simon cannot elude this mandate; he is the

---

[240] Cf. Mk 14:29.

[241] The Psalmist says of David: "With upright heart he tended them, and guided them with skillful hand" (Ps 78: 72). Perhaps the fact that he was a shepherd made the imagery more fitting for the monarch. Moses and Aaron also guided "the people as a flock" (Ps 77:21). God called Cyrus: "Shepherd of mine" (Is 44:28).

The image of the "shepherd" has particular relevance in the Old Testament: God is presented as the Shepherd of Israel (cf. Gn 48:15; 49:24; Hos 4:16; Micah 7:14; Ps 80:2); he frees and leads his flock (cf. Is 40:11; 63:11; Ps 76:21; 78:52-53); he entrusts the flockt to pastors he chooses (cf. 2 Sam 5:2; Jer 10:21; Is 63:11; Ps 78:71-72); he admonishes unfaithful shepherds (cf. Jer 23:1-2; 50:17-18; Ezech 34; Zech 11:4-5); he punishes and scatters the flock among all other peoples (cf. Ps 44:12, 23; 74:1); he gathers and watches over the flock with love (cf. Mic 2:12; 4:6-7; Soph 3: 19); and he promises a good shepherd (cf. Ezech 20:37; 34:23-24; Micah 5:3).

guarantor of the flock's security. After Jesus' example, he is to be the "Good Shepherd," always ready to give his life for the sheep.[242] Without the shepherd, the sheep scatter and grow weak, as Jesus expressly stated.[243] There must be one flock and one shepherd.[244]

On the basis of the Christ-given task comes Peter's heartfelt appeal in his first letter to the "elders," namely, those responsible for the Christian community: "Tend the flock of God that is your charge, not by constraint but willingly, not for shameful gain but eagerly, not as domineering over those in your charge but being examples to the flock. And when the chief Shepherd is manifested you will obtain the unfading crown of glory."[245]

The third account of the apparition of the Risen Christ on Lake Tiberias has a brief conversation between Jesus and Peter.

Jesus says to Peter: "When you were young, you girded yourself and walked where you would; but when you are old, you will stretch out your hands, and another will gird you and carry you where you do not wish to go." These mysterious words are explained by the Evangelist: "This he said to show by what death he was to glorify God," Tradition has seen in this prophecy not only a prediction that Peter would suffer a martyr's death, but also the manner in which he would be martyred, namely, crucifixion.

The Master then turns to the disciple to whom he has just entrusted his flock and says to him:

---

[242] Cf. Jn 10:11, 14.
[243] Cf. Mt 9:36.
[244] Cf. Jn 10:16.
[245] 1 Pt 5:2-4.

"Follow me!" Though brief and unspecific, the call can certainly imply the idea of following Christ to his death, reminiscent of Peter's words at the Last Supper: "*Lord, why cannot I follow you now? I will lay down my life for you.*"[246]

Once again, Jesus calls upon Peter to follow him. A first time, Jesus called him so as to make him a "fisher of men," then he followed him immediately.[247] However, at that time, he did not understand that following Christ meant losing one's life for his sake,[248] and thus, he advised Jesus to avoid the suffering which awaited him.[249] Following the example of his Master, he must now lose his life to save it.[250]

Jesus' call to follow him instinctively makes Peter aware that "the disciple whom Jesus loved" is also present and he displays a particular interest in his future, prompting the question: "*Lord, what about this man?*" But, the Master does not reveal the destiny of the unnamed disciple, because it ought not to be of interest to him: "*If it is my will that he remain until I come, what is that to you?*"[251] What matters for Peter is to follow the Master, who concludes the conversation by saying to him a third time: "Follow me!" Peter enters and leaves this Gospel scene hearing this call.

---

[246] Jn 13:36-37.
[247] Cf. Mt 4:18-20; Mk 1:16-18; Lk 5:19.
[248] Cf. Lk 21:16.
[249] Cf. Mt 16:21-25.
[250] Cf. Lk 17:33; Jn 12:25.
[251] John states that "the saying spread abroad among the brethren that this disciple was not to die," and specifies that "Jesus did not say to him that he was not to die, but 'if it is my will that he remain until I come, what is that to you?'" (21:23).

11. "For we cannot but speak of all we have seen and heard" [252]

In *Acts of the Apostles* Luke gives an account of the work of certain Apostles, primarily Peter and Paul and, in an incidental way, James and John. His presentation is centred on the Church gathered around Peter and growing, especially through Paul's missionary efforts, throughout the Roman Empire, understood at that time to mean the entire civilized world. [253]

Peter heads the list of Apostles who "devoted themselves with one accord to prayer, together with the women and Mary the mother of Jesus, and with his brethren." [254]

Before ascending into heaven, Jesus entrusts to Peter and the other Apostles the mandate of continuing the work of salvation which he began: "Go into all the world and preach the Gospel to the whole creation." [255] "You shall be my witnesses in Jerusalem and in all Judea and Samaria and to the end of the earth." [256] They shall be "witnesses" of what the Master "did and taught." Thus concludes the earthly activity of Jesus and the time of the Church begins.

To fulfill their mandate, the Apostles' first act is to find a substitute for Judas. Peter sets the criteria for the choice: "*He is to be one of the men*

---

[252] Acts 4:20.

[253] In *Acts of the Apostles* Luke traces the Gospel's journey from Peter and Jerusalem (cf. Acts 1-15) to Paul and the Churches of Asia Minor, Greece and Rome (cf. Acts 16-28).

[254] Acts 1:14.

[255] Mk 16:15.

[256] Acts 1:1.8.

who have accompanied us during all the time that the Lord Jesus went in and out among us, beginning from the baptism of John until the day when he was taken up from us – one of these men must become with us a witness to his reusrrection."

After the descent of the Holy Spirit on the Apostles,[257] Peter, speaks for the Twelve, declaring them to be witnesses of the Resurrection.[258] He also gives a solemn discourse which is the first great proclamation of Jesus' Resurrection.

Peter, "standing up and lifting up his voice" addresses "devout Jews from every nation under heaven," who were gathered in Jerusalem and from the Diaspora for the celebrations related to Passover. After using Sacred Scripture to offer an explanation of what happened at Pentecost, he shows that Jesus is Messiah and risen from the dead. He "boldly" (*metà parresías*) levels an accusation against the Jews: "You crucified and killed him by the hands of lawless men." More insistently, he accuses them again: "Let all the house of Israel therefore know assuredly that God has made him both Lord and Christ, this Jesus whom you crucified."

His listeners are "awe-struck" at his words. Peter then calls upon them to repent and be converted. Luke describes the psychological effect of Peter's discourse: the Jews "heard this and were cut to the heart;" he also records the number of conversions: "Those who received his word were baptized, and there were added that day about three thousand souls."[259]

---

257 Cf. Acts 2:1-4.
258 Cf. Acts 2:32.
259 Cf. Acts 2:14-41.

Thus the Church expands under the impulse of the Holy Spirit and through Peter's preaching.

In Acts, Luke often has John accompany Peter, almost like his "shadow;" however, Peter is always the leading character. They are first found together, going up to the temple to pray. A lame man asks them for alms. Peter says to him: "*I have no gold or silver, but I give you what I have; in the name of Jesus Christ of Nazareth, walk!*" And the beggar was healed.[260]

If courage (*parresía*) means feeling free to speak the truth in one's heart, Peter takes advantage of the occasion to speak to the people, who are amazed at the miracle.[261]

After insisting that God alone was the source of the healing of the lame man, Peter has the courage to attribute, again for a third time, the killing of Jesus to the Jews: "*The God of our fathers, glorified his servant Jesus, whom you delivered up and denied in the presence of Pilate, when he had decided to release him. But you denied the Holy and Righteous One, and asked for a murderer to be granted to you, and killed the Author of life, whom God raised from the dead. To this we are witnesses.*"

Peter then appeals to them to repent. To make their conversion easier, he offers an excuse for their action: "*Now, brethren, I know that you acted out of ignorance, as did your rulers;*" and engenders trust in their hearts by assuring them: "*God, having raised up his servant (Jesus), sent him to you first, to bless you in turning every one of you from your wickedness.*"

---

[260] Cf. Acts 3:1-10.
[261] Cf. Acts 3:11-26.

Luke again precisely records the effect of this discourse: "Many of those who heard the word believed; and the number of the men came to about five thousand."[262]

If courage is the refusal to act in any type of a faint-hearted manner or out of consideration for another's power or position, Peter is an indisputable example of such courage before the Sanhedrin.[263]

The religious authorities, "annoyed because they (Peter and John) were teaching the people and proclaiming in Jesus the resurrection of the dead, have Peter and John arrested.

The trial takes place the following day before the high authorities.[264] But Peter is not cowered and repeats the essential doctrinal points of Christianity: "*By the name of Jesus Christ of Nazareth, whom you crucified, whom God raised from the dead,*[265] *by him this man is standing before you well. This is the stone which was rejected by you builders, but which has become the head of the corner* [namely the foundation of the new Christian community]. *There is salvation in no one else, for there is no other name under heaven given among men by which we must be saved.*"

The "judges" were surprised at the boldness (*parressía*) with which these two people, who were

---

[262] Cf. Acts 4:4.

[263] Cf. Acts 4:1-22.

[264] Luke lists the authorities who were present for the trial, almost to highlight Peter's courage: "Rulers and elders and scribes were gathered together in Jerusalem, with Annas the high priest and Caiaphas and John and Alexander, and all who were of the high-priestly family" (Acts 4:5-6).

[265] This is the fourth time Peter dares to attribute Jesus' death to the Jews; he will do it for a fifth time in his discourse to Cornelius the centurion (cf. Acts 10:40).

"uneducated (*agrámmatoi*) and common men (*idiôtai*)", proclaimed the Gospel and ordered them "to speak no more to any one in this name."

They refused to accept such a prohibition and dared to challenge the Sanhedrin: *"Whether it is right in the sight of God to listen to you rather than to God, you must judge; for we cannot but speak of what we have seen and heard."*

Witnesses ("martyrs") of the Gospel have only one choice: disobedience to men and obedience to God. Thus Peter and John do not fear threats, as illustrated in the prayer which they say together for the first Christian community: "Lord, look upon their threats, and grant to thy servants to speak thy word with boldness (*parresía*)."[266]

The account concludes with a new Pentecost and the gift of courage in preaching: "All were filled with the Holy Spirit and spoke the word of God with boldness (*parresía*)."[267]

Under the influence of the Holy Spirit, the first community, "those who believed, were of one heart and soul, and no one said that any of the things which he possessed was his own, but they had everything in common. There was not a needy person among them, for as many as were possessors of lands or houses sold them, and brought the proceeds of what was sold and laid it at the Apostles' feet; and distribution was made to each as any had need."[268]

Peter guided the Christian community and was responsible in disciplinary matters. This is clearly seen in the episode of Ananias and

---

[266] Acts 4:29.
[267] Acts 4:31.
[268] Acts 4:32, 34; cf. 2:44.

Sapphira, a married couple who did not respect the traditions of the first Christian community to which they had freely chosen to belong.

The couple tried to defraud the community, giving only a part of the sum of money received at the sale of their property. Peter, on behalf of the Apostles, judges their deed. He bitterly reproaches the husband first, and then the wife, because "they lied not to men but to God." For this, God punished them with an instant death.[269]

The Apostles' principal activity was that of witnessing to the Risen Christ through their preaching. When it comes to their attention that some of the needs of the community, like service to the poor, encroach on the proclamation of the Gospel, they institute deacons, because "*it is not right that we should give up preaching the word of God to serve tables.*"[270] Luke does not say if they were present for the election of these deacons, but it can reasonably be assumed that Peter might have been present.

Jesus warned the Apostles that the proclamation of the Gospel would lead to their being persecuted: "They will deliver you up to councils; and you will be beaten in synagogues; and you will stand before governors and kings for my sake, to bear witness before them. ... You will be hated by all for my name's sake. But he who endures to the end will be saved."[271]

Jesus' prediction becomes a cruel reality. Peter and John are arrested a second time, but an Angel opens the doors of prison and sends them forth

---

[269] Cf. Acts 5:1-11.
[270] Acts 6:2.
[271] Mk 13:9, 13; cf. Mt 10:17-23; Lk 21:12-19.

to preach to the people in the Temple, where they are again arrested and led before the Sanhedrin.

The high priest tells them that they have disobeyed their orders no longer to speak in the name of Jesus. With a persuasiveness that does not depend on skill with words but faith in God, Peter again emphasizes the choice which he previously made with John, when the Sanhedrin had forbade them to preach: "*We must obey God rather than men. The God of our fathers raised Jesus whom you killed by hanging him on a tree. God exalted him at his right hand as Leader and Saviour, to give repentance to Israel and forgiveness of sins.*" And he adds: "*And we are witnesses to these things, and so is the Holy Spirit whom God has given to those who obey him.*"

Peter's words so annoy the religious authorities that they would have them put to death, if it were not for the intervention of Gamaliel: "Keep away from these men and let them alone; for if this plan or this undertaking is of men, it will fail; but if it is of God, you will not be able to overthrow them. You might even be found opposing God!"

The sage advise of Gamaliel was accepted and the two Apostles, after being flogged, were allowed to go free. Luke describes their state of mind: "Then they left the presence of the council, rejoicing that they were counted worthy to suffer dishonour for the name."[272]

Peter also has a determinant role in the spread of the Gospel.

The Apostles send Peter and John from Jerusalem to Samaria to complete the evangeliza-

---

[272] Cf. Acts 5:17-41.

tion started by the deacon Philip. Their task is that of praying that the Samaritans "might receive the Holy Spirit," given that the Holy Spirit "had not yet fallen on any of them; they had only been baptized in the name of the Lord Jesus."

Present at the event was a man called Simon, "the magician" who was baptized by Philip. When he "saw that the Spirit was given through the laying on of the apostles' hands," Simon offered money to Peter and John, saying, "give me also this power." Simon sought to buy the apostolic office and its prerogatives, thinking that the imposition of hands was a magical art to bestow the Holy Spirit.

Even though the request is made to both Apostles, Peter alone speaks: *"Your silver perish with you, because you thought you could obtain the gift of God with money! You have neither part nor lot in this matter, for your heart is not right before God. Repent therefore of this wickedness of yours, and pray to the Lord that, if possible, the intent of your heart may be forgiven you."*[273]

Concluding the narrative of the Peter and John's mission in Samaria, Luke makes explicit reference to the spread of the Gospel and the birth of local Churches: "Now when they had testified and spoken the word of the Lord, they returned to Jerusalem, preaching the Gospel to many villages of the Samaritans."

Peter was not afraid to proclaim the Gospel wherever he was, in whatever circumstance and in whatever manner. His "Christological discourses" in Acts[274] illustrate his courage. He became a new

---

[273] Cf. Acts 8:9-25.
[274] Cf. Acts 2:22-36; 3:11-26; 4:8-12; 10:34-43; 13:16-41.

person who bore witness to Jesus in a clear and straightforward way; by now he had overcome all the fear which he and the other Apostles displayed in the course of Jesus' Passion.[275]

Where Luke might have elaborated on Peter's activities from a pastoral point of view, this does not alter the objective nature of the facts.

God accompanied the preaching of the Apostles with "many miracles and signs."[276] As for the miraculous powers attributed to Peter, Luke states that "they even carried out the sick into the streets, and laid them on beds and pallets, that as Peter came by his shadow might fall on some of them."[277]

Among the miracles performed by Peter, Acts records – besides that of the lame man who begs alms at the Temple gate – the cure of the man of Lydda who had been paralyzed for eight years to whom he commands: *"Aeneus, Jesus Christ heals you; rise and make your bed!"*; and the woman at Joppa, full of good works, who was returned to life at the Apostle's command: *"Tabitha, rise!"*.

Two miracles are narrated by Luke with the specific intention of presenting Peter as missionary and apostolic visitor to the first Christian communities. This can be intimated from the introduction to the healing of Aeneas: "And as Peter went here and there among them all, he came down also to the saints that lived in Lydda."[278]

---

[275] Cf. Mt 14:30; Mk 4:40; Mt 26:56; Mk 14:50.
[276] Acts 5:12.
[277] Acts 5:15.
[278] Cf .Acts 9:32-42.

The first Christian community had periods of "peace," in which it was "built up; and walking in the fear of the Lord and in the comfort of the Holy Spirit, it was multiplied;"[279] it also had periods of persecution, like that in which Herod Agrippa I persecuted some of the Church's members and killed James (called the Greater), brother of John; and that of 42 A.D. in which Peter was arrested, "when he saw that this pleased the Jews." This is Peter's third arrest.

Peter is in prison, bound with two chains with four squads of soldiers to guard him; he is awaiting a trial which will turn into a spectacle, because of the great masses of people who gathered in Jerusalem at the end of Passover. All the while, "earnest prayer for him was made to God for him by the Church."

God hears the prayer of the community and sends an Angel to free the Apostle. At first he thinks he is dreaming. However, when he comes to his senses, he understands that he was freed through divine intervention: "*Now I am sure that the Lord has sent his angel and rescued me from the hand of Herod and from all that the Jewish people were expecting!*".

Peter's miraculous liberation from prison causes "joy" and "wonder" in the community which is united in prayer. He then recounts how it came about and says to them: "*Tell this to James and to the brethren.*"[280]

---

[279] Acts 9:31.
[280] Cf. Acts 12:1-19. James "the brother of the Lord" was a leader of the Jewish-Christian community in Jerusalem at the time Paul made his first visit, about 36 A.D. (cf. Gal 1:19). He was a leading figure at the "Council of Jerusalem."

The Martyrdom of St. Peter
Michelangelo
Pauline Chapel, Vatican City.

The Crucifixion of St. Peter
Guido Reni
Painting Gallery, Vatican City.

12. "God made choice among you, that by my mouth the Gentiles should hear the word of the Gospel" [281]

In the account of Cornelius the centurion – the longest narrative in the *Acts of the Apostles*[282] – Peter is not only the first evangelizer of the Jews,[283] but also of the Gentiles.

He initially entertains doubts, which are quickly resolved in an act of trustful abandon to God's will.

Peter enters the house of the Roman centurion Cornelius, "an upright and God fearing man," where he makes the following observations on Jesus activities: "*He went about doing good and healing all that were oppressed by the devil for God was with him*"; he was put to death by the Jews; he was raised to life on the third day and appeared "*not to all people, but to us who were chosen by God as witnesses.*"

---

[281] Acts 15:7.

[282] Cf. Acts 10:9-48. Before Peter, *Acts of the Apostles* records conversions which happened outside Judaism, for example, the deacon Philip converts many Samaritans through his preaching and baptizes the Ethiopian eunuch (8:5-8, 26-40).

[283] Paul states: "I had been entrusted with the Gospel to the uncircumcised, as Peter had been entrusted with the Gospel to the circumcised" (Gal 2:7). Such an affirmation seems to stand in contrast to Peter's initiative of baptizing the first unbeliever and with his declaration of having been chosen by God to evangelize Gentiles (cf. Acts 15:7). The difficulty is resolved, if one considers that chapters 10 and 11 of Acts are composed by Luke who, because of the importance of Peter in relation to the other Apostles, theologically saw fit to entrust to Peter the first act of the evangelization of the Gentiles.

Peter announces the second principle: that all men indiscriminately can be followers of Christ: "*God shows no partiality, but in every nation any one who fears him and does what is right is acceptable to him. ... every one who believes in him receives forgiveness of sins through his name.*" Finally, he baptizes Cornelius with all his family.

The circumcision party of Jerusalem, who reproached Peter for entering the house of uncircumcized men and for eating with them, is satisfied with his explanation and approves of his conduct. They "begin to glorify God, saying: 'then to the Gentiles also God has granted repentance unto life'."[284]

Thus Peter, reaffirming the Christians' liberation from the weight of Jewish traditions, assists the spread of the Gospel in the Gentile world and opens a new chapter in the religious story of humanity.

In Antioch, where a great number of Greeks believed and were converted to the Lord[285] and where Jesus' first disciples were called "Christians,"[286] the problem arises as to whether the Gentiles need to submit to circumcision and Jewish laws and customs. Some, coming to Antioch from Jerusalem, "taught: 'Unless you are circumcised according to the custom of Moses, you cannot be saved.'"[287] Paul and Barnabas, however, who preached in Antioch,

---

[284] Acts 11:1-3, 18.

[285] Cf. Acts 11:20-21.

[286] Acts 11:26.

[287] These were called Judaizers for their attachment to Jewish traditions.

"had no small dissension and debate with them."[288]

The solution to the problem of the evangelization of Gentiles for the first group was in uniting the law and the Gospel; for the other groups, one excluded the other; it was either Christ or the Law. The seemingly irreconcilable problem was primarily on circumcision. The Judaizers, whom Paul calls "false brethren,"[289] held that without circumcison there was no salvation; on the contrary, Paul holds that those who are circumcised are excluded from salvation.[290]

To settle the matter, "Paul and Barnabas and some of the others were appointed to go to Jerusalem to the Apostles and elders."[291] Paul, as he had already done after his conversion,[292]

---

[288] Acts 15:1-2.

[289] Gal 2:4. Such expressions demonstrate the intrangient attitude of the Judaizers, before whom he did not yield "even for a moment, that the truth of the Gospel might remain intact" (Gal 2:5).

[290] Cf. Gal 5:2.

[291] Acts 15:2.

[292] Acts states that Paul, after his conversion, came to Jerusalem; "he attempted to join the disciples; and they were all afraid of him, for they did not believe that he was a disciple. But Barnabas took him, and brought him to the Apostles, and declared to them how on the road he had seen the Lord, who spoke too him, and how at Damascus, he had preached boldly in the name of Jesus . So he went in and out among them at Jerusalem" (Acts 9:26-28). In the Letter to the Galatians Paul recounts the same visit, made about 37-38 A.D., three years after his conversion, for the purpose of "consulting (istorLsai) Cephas." He ramained 15 days, during which he did not meet with any other Apostle, except James (cf. 1:18-19). Given that the word istoreîn (appearing only here in the New Testament) means in classical Greek "to seek," or "to interrogate" an expert

wants to confer with "James, Cephas and John, who were reputed to be pillars of the Church"[293] to avoid the risk of "running in vain,"[294] and fully aware that "he who worked through Peter for the mission to the circumcised worked through him also for the Gentiles."[295]

The assembly, called "the Council of Jerusalem" or "the Council of Apostles" is divided, but in the end a solution is accepted by all.[296]

---

or an historian (*istór*), it can reasonably be presumed that Paul asked Peter what Jesus had said and done.

[293] Gal 2:9.

[294] Gal 2:2.

[295] Gal 2:8.

[296] The Council at Jerusalem is narrated by Paul (cf. Gal 2:1-10) and Luke (cf. Acts 15:1-29). We do not know with certainty if the two accounts refer to the same event or two separate ones, given some differences in the two texts. The following are examples: a) In the Letter to the Galatians the meeting takes place during the second visit of Paul to Jerusalem (he speaks of only two visits: one after his conversion, cf. Gal 1:18; the other for the "Council", cf. Gal 2:1) and he goes there "following a revelation," and not on the occasion of the third visit, when he is sent by the Church in Antioch, as recorded in Acts (for Luke the first visit is immediately after his conversion, cf. 9:26; the second when he goes with Barnabas to bring the collection, cf. 11:30; 12:25; the third for the "Council," cf. 15:2); b) Paul does not mention the important "Apostolic Letter," which according to Acts is sent "to the brethren of Antioch, Syria and Cilicia." He does not mention the clause of James concerning converted Gentiles, but, in this regard, he says he has received only one recommendation: "Only they would have us remember the poor" (Gal 2:10). Some consider this the same event, given the similarities of the two accounts: the place where the assembly takes place, the persons involved, the subject matter treated and the same solution to the problem. The differences could be a result of the different perspectives and purposes of the two authors who narrated the same event. Paul was

One side, "some believers who belonged to the party of the Pharisees, rose up and said, 'It is necessary to circumcise them, and to charge them to keep the law of Moses.'"[297]

For the other side, Peter speaks – his last words in the New Testament – as the spokeman for the Apostles. He makes a direct reference to the conversion of Cornelius.

He first addresses all Christians present: "*Brethren, you know that in the early days God made choice among you, that by my mouth the Gentiles should hear the word of the gospel and believe. And God who knows the heart bore witness to them, giving them the Holy Spirit just as he did to us; and he made no distinction between us and them, but cleansed their hearts by faith.*"

Then he speaks to the Judaizers: "*Now therefore why do you make trial of God by putting a yoke upon the neck of the disciples which neither our fathers nor we have been able to bear? But we believe that we shall be saved through the grace of the Lord Jesus, just as they will.*"[298]

Peter's discourse convinced the entire assembly, which "kept silence;" His words served as a preparation for the speeches of Paul and Barnabas, who limited themselves to "relating what signs and wonders God had done through them among the Gentiles."[299]

---

interested primarily in the decision of the assembly and left aside the details which did not interest him; furthermore, he presents the facts in a personal literary style significantly different from that of Luke.

[297] Acts 15:5.
[298] Acts 15:7-11.
[299] Acts 15:12.

Paul and Barnabas' interventions lend credence to Peter's discourse. Indeed, they can be said to be the decisive proof, because miracles mean that God confirms what the two missionaries are doing in their work of evangelizing the Gentiles.

James has the last word at the assembly. He supports what Peter said, but adds: "My judgment is that we should not trouble those of the Gentiles who turn to God." However, out of respect for the sensibilities of the Judaizers,[300] he proposes the following injunction: "They are to abstain from the pollutions of idols and from unchastity and from what is strangled and from blood."[301]

---

[300] Paul also voices his concern not to harm the religious sensibilities of the brethren. He exhorts the Corinthians to take care that "their liberty somehow become a stumbling block to the weak." He cites as an example the case of flesh offered to idols, permitted to be eaten by Christians but forbidden to the Jews. In this regard he states: "If food is the cause of my brother's falling, I will never eat meat, lest I cause my brother to fall" (1 Cor 8:7-13). He also expresses his pastoral reasoning: "For though I am free from all men, I have made myself a slave to all, that I might win the more. To the Jews I became as a Jew, in order to win Jews; to those under the law I became as one under the law – though not being myself under the law – that I might win those under the law. To those outside the law I became as one outside the law – not being without law toward God but under the law of Christ – that I might win those outside the law" (1 Cor 9:19-21).

[301] The question concerns attitudes which come from the cultural laws of the Old Testament. The expression "uncleanliness of idols" refers to the prohibition of eating the flesh of animals sacrificed to pagan gods; "immodesty" is a reference to the irregular unions listed in Lev 18:6-18; the clause "suffocated animals" refers to the law prohibiting eating the flesh of animals who were "suffocated," or ani-

The injunctions given by James leave little doubt that the idea of ritual purity was a problem for Christians of both Jewish and Gentile origin. The former did not wish to break with their glorious tradition; the latter could not forget that eating flesh offered to idols in pagan rites was wrong. In this regard, Paul writes: "Some, though being hitherto accustomed to idols, eat food as really offered to an idol; and their conscience being weak, is defiled."[302]

The decision was made that Gentiles who converted to the Gospel were free of the obligation to observe the precepts of the Mosaic Law, and, under the guidance of the Holy Spirit, the Assembly unanimously agreed to the injunction given by James. The whole matter was then reported in a letter addressed to the brethren of Antioch, Syria and Cilicia, who "rejoice at the encouragement it gave."[303]

According to the Letter to the Galatians, James, Cephas and John gave "the right hand of fellowship" to Paul and Barnabas during the Assembly at Jerusalem.[304] At the same time, he tells of a discussion which took place related to Peter's conduct in the matter at hand: "When Cephas came to Antioch I opposed him to his face, because he stood condemned. For before

---

mals who die of natural causes, that is, not butchered (cf. Ex 22:30; Lev 17:15; Deut 14:21); and "abstaining from blood" concerns the prohibition of eating anything containing blood or foods prepared in whole or in part with blood in them. (cf. Lev 17;10, 12).

[302] 1 Cor 8:7.

[303] Cf. Acts 15:22-32.

[304] Cf. Gal 2:9.

certain men came from James, he ate with the Gentiles; but when they came he drew back and separated himself, fearing the circumcision party. And with him the rest of the Jews acted insincerely, so that even Barnabas was carried away by their insincerity. But when I saw that they were not straightforward about the truth of the Gospel, I said to Cephas before them all, 'If you, though a Jew, live like a Gentile and not like a Jew, how can you compel the Gentiles to live like Jews?'."[305]

Having said this, it must also be pointed out that Paul also acted in the same manner as Peter. Take for example the case of Timothy, the son of "of a Jewish woman who was a believer and a Greek father." Paul has him "circumcised because of the Jews.[306] He justifies his conduct in the name of charity.[307] However, Peter's case can create two problems. People could think that only converted Jews who observe the law are authentic Christians, which, in turn, could give rise to two completely different communities in the Church.

Apart from these dangers, the fact remains that Peter "put aside" his true convictions at a time he was obliged to show them. In this way, he is seen as weak, ambiguous and a coward. Because of the authority which he enjoyed amidst the community, he is unaware that his behaviour could lead others to do the same, as in the case of Barnabas.

---

[305] Gal 2:11-14.
[306] At 16:1, 3.
[307] Cf. Acts 21:26; 1 Cor 8:13; 9:20-22; Rm 14:21.

The incident at Antioch had absolutely no effect on the fellowship between the two Apostles.

The "Council of Jerusalem" concludes the "life story" of Peter, as recorded in *Acts of the Apostles.*[308]

---

[308] According to historic, patristic and apocryphal tradition, Peter spent the last years of his life in Rome (a good 25 years!), where he died a martyr about 64-67 A.D., according to Clement of Rome, who wrote about 95 A.D., (cf. *1 Clemente* 5:2-7) and Ignatius (*Romani* 4:3), a martyr under the reign of Trajan (98-117 A.D.). Tertullian (circa 160-220 A.D.) states that Peter was crucified (*Scorpiace*, 15:3); Origen (+ 253-254), cited by Eusebius of Cesarea (circa 265-339 A.D.), says that "he was crucified upside-down in Rome, after having asked to suffer in this manner" (*Historia ecclesiastica*, 3, I, 2: PG 20, 216). This tradition was most probably taken from *Acts of Peter*, written in approximately 180-190 A.D., which states: "The soldiers then took St. Peter, and when they reached the place of crucifixion, the blessed Peter said to them: 'My Lord Jesus Christ, come down from heaven to earth, was crucified upright on a cross, since he now sees fit to call me from earth to heaven, my cross ought to be planted with the head downwards, so that I can set me feet towards heaven. In fact, I am not worthy to be crucified as my Lord was.' They turned the cross upside-down and nailed his feet upwards." (81; cf. 37).

The Apostle was buried on Vatican hill. Over his tomb, the Emperor Constantine had a basilica built in his honour. 26 June 1968, Pope Paul VI announced that the bones from the pre-Constantinian necropolis, under the Basilica, were those of Peter.

13. "In this you rejoice, though now for a little while you may have to suffer various trials" [309]

The description of Peter's human and spiritual composition is completed by two letters which are attributed to him. [310]

In his first letter, Peter appeals to the people to be saints, gathered together around Christ, "the living stone." They are to be "living stones built into a spiritual house." Peter then enunciates the central theme of his letter: "In this you

---

[309] 1 Pt 1: 6.

[310] Tradition has always attributed the authorship of the First Letter to Peter who presents himself as the "Apostle of Jesus Christ" (1:1), "an elder (*presbýteros*)", namely one entrusted with tending God's flock, and "witness to the sufferings of Christ" (5:1). The Letter was written from Rome (with the code name 'Babylon'), where he is with Mark (5:13), before his death in 64 or 67 A.D.. Silvano probably assisted him in drafting it (5:12). The Letter is intended for the Christian Diaspora in Asia Minor (1:1), mainly coming from paganism (cf. 1:14-16; 2:10; 4: 3), who live in a strong hostile environment.

The Second Letter of Peter had difficult time before its inclusion in the universally accepted canon of inspired books (decreed on 8 April 1546 by the Council of Trent). Some indications favouring Petrine authorship are: the letter opens with the name of the Apostle (cf. 1:1); an allusion is made to his death (cf. 1:14); he states that he was a witness of the Transfiguration (cf. 1:16-18); and mention is made of a first letter (cf. 3:1), which could be the First Letter of Peter. Factors which argue against Peter's authorship face difficulties. One comes from the literary style of the letter and its relation to the Letter of Jude (of the 25 verses composing the letter, at least 15 appear directly or indirectly in the Second Letter of Peter; it is

rejoice, though now for a little while you may have to suffer various trials."

Every follower of Christ must know that suffering is a school where the authenticity of one's faith is tried: "The genuineness of our faith, more precious than gold which though perishable is tested by fire, may redound to praise and glory and honour."[311]

Suffering is a source of true joy: "But rejoice in so far as you share Christ's sufferings, that you may also rejoice and be glad when his glory is revealed. If you are reproached for the name of Christ, you are blessed, because the spirit of glory and of God rests upon you. But let none of you suffer as a murderer, or a thief, or a wrongdoer, or a mischief-maker; yet if one suffers as a Christian, let him not be ashamed, but under that name let him glorify God. For the time has come for judgment to begin with the household of God; and if it begins with us, what will be the end of those who do not obey the gospel of God? And 'If the righteous man is scarcely saved, where will the impious and sinner appear?' Therefore let those who suffer

not known which was written first, or if both depend on a third source). For this reason, some studies date the letter between the end of the first century and the beginning of the second; some argue that the true author is a disciple of Peter or a Jewish Christian of Greek background who attributes it to Peter to give the work a certain authority. It is unknown whether it is intended for Jews or Gentiles. If it is Peter's, it was written from Rome shortly before his martyrdom (cf. 1:15); Rome remains the most probable origin of the Letter, even if not written by Peter.

[311] 1 Pt 1: 6-7.

according to God's will do right and entrust their souls to a faithful Creator."[312]

Peter points out that no matter what the situation in life, whether dealing with those in authority,[313] with masters,[314] in the family,[315] in the relations between pastors and the faithful,[316] and between the young and old,[317] the focal point must always be Christ's example: "For to this you have been called, because Christ also suffered for you, leaving you an example, that you should follow in his steps. He committed no sin; no guile was found on his lips. When he was reviled, he did not revile in return; when he suffered, he did not threaten; but he trusted to him who judges justly. He himself bore our sins in his body on the tree, that we might die to sin and live to righteousness. By his wounds you have been healed. For you were straying like sheep, but have now returned to the Shepherd and Guardian of your souls."[318]

Suffering becomes a "grace" (*cháris*), if it has the example of Christ as a reference point: "For one is approved if, mindful of God, he endures pain while suffering unjustly. For what credit is it, if when you do wrong and are beaten for it you take it patiently? But if when you do right and suffer for it you take it patiently, you have God's approval."[319]

---

[312] 1 Pt 4:13-19; cf. 2:12; 3:14, 16, 18; 4:1, 5, 9.
[313] Cf. 1 Pt 2:13-17.
[314] Cf. 1 Pt 2:18-20.
[315] Cf. 1 Pt 3:1-7.
[316] Cf. 1 Pt 5:1-4.
[317] Cf. 1 Pt 5:5-7.
[318] 1 Pt 2:21-25.
[319] 1 Pt 2:19-25.

Oftentimes the uprightness of a Christian's life can be the cause of criticism[320] and abuse.[321] Peter indicates the way to treat these trials: "Finally, all of you, have unity of spirit, sympathy, love of the brethren, a tender heart and a humble mind. Do not return evil for evil or reviling for reviling; but on the contrary bless, for to this you have been called, that you may obtain a blessing."[322]

If the Christian acts in this manner, they that "accuse as wrongdoers" will suffer wrong for their wrongdoing.[323] This is the only way to respond to someone who asks "the reason for our hope," namely, one must render one's faith believable.[324]

Peter concludes the first letter, appealing to his readers to be watchful and strong: "Be sober, be watchful. Your adversary the devil prowls around like a roaring lion, seeking some one to devour. Resist him, firm in your faith, knowing that the same experience of suffering is required of your brotherhood throughout the world. And after you have suffered a little while, the God of all grace, who has called you to his eternal glory in Christ, will himself restore, establish, and strengthen you."[325]

In his Second Letter, Peter recalls that every Christian, in virtue of Baptism, shares in the divine nature. After appealing to his readers

---

[320] Cf. 1 Pt 2:12; 3:16.
[321] Cf. 1 Pt 4:4.
[322] 1 Pt 3:8-9.
[323] Cf. 1 Pt 2:12.
[324] Cf. 1 Pt 3:15.
[325] 1 Pt 5: 8-10.

to enrich their faith with the virtues of the Christian life,[326] he returns to the theme of vigilance and perseverance, so as not "to be disturbed by the wrongs of the impious."[327]

He calls for this because there are "false prophets among the people," "false teachers" who sow the seeds of "destructive heresies, even denying the Master who bought them." A severe warning is directed to "bold and wilful" people, who through their conduct of life are similar to "irrational animals." He says that they "will be destroyed in their corruption, suffering wrong for their wrongdoing."[328]

As for what concerns the Lord's coming (*parousía*), he tells them not to believe in "cleverly devised myths;" they are to adhere to the word of the Prophets, which is "like a lamp shining in a dark place, until the day dawns and the morning star rises in their hearts." In this regard, he states that "no prophecy of Scripture is a matter of one's own interpretation, because no prophecy ever came by the impulse of man, but men moved by the Holy Spirit spoke from God." [329]

The "scoffers," who put into doubt the Lord's coming, need to remember that man's notion of time is not God's notion of time: "with the Lord one day is as a thousand years, and a thousand years as one day." It is certain that "the Lord is not slow about his promise as

---

[326] Cf. 2 Pt 1:3-11.
[327] 2 Pt 3:11-18.
[328] Cf 2 Pt 2:1-22.
[329] Cf. 2 Pt 1:16-21.

some count slowness, but is forbearing toward you, not wishing that any should perish, but that all should reach repentance." However, it is necessary always to be watchful, because "the day of the Lord will come like a thief."[330]

[330] Cf. 2 Pt 3:3-10.

The Martyrdom of St. Peter
Detail, Stefaneschi Triptych
Painting Gallery, Vatican City.

The Crucifixion of St. Peter
Filarete
Bronze Doors of St. Peter's Basilica, Vatican City.

Conclusion

We have clearly seen that the New Testament amply shows the spiritual development of the Apostle Peter.

When Jesus calls him, he immediately leaves everything to follow him, but shortly thereafter he wants to know what he will receive in return.[331]

Except for some rare moments when the Father reveals that Jesus is the "Christ, the Son of the living God"[332] and "the Holy One of God,"[333] Peter perceives his Master to be the long-awaited Messah-King who is to restore the temporal kingdom of Israel.[334] On the basis of this conviction, when Jesus announces his Passion, he "reproaches" him and tells him to avoid suffering.[335] Moreover, the Apostles discuss who will be the greatest in the kingdom to come,[336] indeed, two dare to ask to occupy the first places.[337]

In accompanying Jesus, Peter shows himself to be impulsive[338] and "a man of little faith."[339] During the Master's Passion, he is unable to stay awake to pray with him;[340] when Jesus is

---

[331] Cf. Mt 19:29; cf. Mk 10:28-31; Lk 18:28-30.
[332] Mt 16:17.
[333] Jn 6:69.
[334] Cf. Acts 1:6.
[335] Cf. Mt 16:21-23; Mk 8:31-33.
[336] Cf. Mt 18:1; Mk 9:33; Lk 9:46.
[337] Cf. Mt 20:20-23; Mk 10:35-40.
[338] Cf. Mt 26:51-52; Jn 13:6-11.
[339] Cf. Mt 14:31.
[340] Cf. Mk 14:37.

arrested, he abandons him;[341] and finally, out of fear of meeting the same end, Peter denies Christ three times,[342] despite having solemnly declared: *"Though they all fall away because of you, I will never fall away... Even if I must die with you, I will not deny you."*[343]

Only after the Resurrection and Pentecost do the Gospels and *Acts of the Apostles* present Peter as radically transformed. Now, he is the Apostle who declares with deep conviction to love his Master most.[344] He boldly (*parresía*) proclaims Christ's Resurrection[345] and is joyous at being mistreated out of love for Jesus' name.[346] After a long life entirely spent in proclaiming the Gospel, Peter doesn't hesitate to lay down his life in testimony to his faith in Christ.

The attractiveness of the figure of Peter comes precisely from his weak nature and unconditional love for his Master. He is the Apostle who denied Christ, but loved him most.

The Church Fathers gave particular attention to these two aspects of Peter's character.

According to St. Chromatius of Aquileia (martyred, 407 A.D.), the unexpected "violence of the wind," which roused fear in Peter, making him sink as he walks on the water

---

[341] Cf. Mt 26:56; Mk 14:50.
[342] Cf. Mt 26:69-75; Mk 14:66-72; Lk 22:55-62; Jn 18:17, 25-27.
[343] Mt 26:33, 35.
[344] Cf. Jn 21:15-17.
[345] Cf. Acts 2:29; 4:13, 29, 31.
[346] Cf. Acts 5:41.

towards Christ,[347] symbolizes "the tempest" in which Peter finds himself when he denies his Master. "In those moments, Peter truly feared and began almost to run the risk of drowning. When asked by a servant girl if he knew Jesus of Nazareth, that is, the Lord Christ, he denied, one, two and three times..., the Son of God, whom he had previously confessed, and to whom he insisted that he would be willing to face even death. Peter, then, is about to drown in this manner; but he cried out to the Lord for help: 'Save me,' and immediately Jesus extended his hand and Peter grasped it. What else ought to be seen in Peter's call for help, if not that, at the point of drowning in denying Christ three times, he cried out with all his heart to the Lord in faith, using his bitter tears?"

The Lord and Saviour, "calms the tempest of persecution," just as he caused the violent wind to cease and the fright of his disciples to subside, "he makes Peter the foundation of the Apostles; he entrusts him with his sheep in an entirely special way, when he said: 'Tend my sheep'"[348].

St. John Chrysostom (345-407 A.D.) highlights both Peter's weak nature and greatness: "The Evangelist did not simply say that 'he (Peter) cried' but 'he cried bitterly.' The

---

[347] Cf. Mt 14:28-32.

[348] St. Chromatius of Aquileia, *Tract 52*, 6-8. St. Hilary of Poitiers (315-367 A.D.) also links this episode with Peter's denial (*Commentary on Matthew*, XIV, 15). Origen, commenting on the same incident, observes that Jesus did not say to Peter: "Disbeliever," but only "Man of little faith" (*Commentary on Matthew*, XI, 6).

expression indicates that the power of those tears is beyond words and is clear proof of what immediately took place after his unhappy fall. No sin could be as serious as Peter's denial. However, even in this case, God allowed him to rise from this tragedy and restored his former honour, giving him authority over the entire Church in world."[349]

Furthermore, St. John Chrysostom clearly indicates the relation between Peter's statement that he loved Christ most and the task, bestowed by Christ, of tending the sheep: "The Master asks Peter if he loves him, not for the knowledge of it (he knows the thoughts of every heart), but to teach us how much Peter has to take to heart the care of the flock. ... He did not intend to show how much Peter loved him (this was already seen in other deeds), but how much Peter loved his Church and to teach Peter and us what is required in this work."[350]

St. Optatus of Milevi (martyred, 385 A.D.) says that, although Peter denied Christ three times, "he does not deserve, for the sake of unity, to be excluded from the group of Apostles." The Saviour gave the keys of the Church to Peter, so that the other Apostles might "not arbitrarily judge and hold in contempt the one who denied Christ. Many innocent people were present, yet the sinner is the one to receive the keys. In this way he determined the dynamic of unity: the sinner opened the doors to the innocent, and the innocent did

---

[349] St. John Chrysostom, *On penitence*, Homily V, 2.
[350] St. John Chrysostom, *On priesthood*, II, 1.

not close the doors to a sinner, and thus unity, an absolute necessity, was achieved."[351]

St. Augustine (354-430 A.D.) underlines how the task of tending the sheep implies the supreme sacrifice of laying down one's life: "'I entrust my sheep to you!' Which sheep? Those that I have bought with my blood. For them I died. 'Do you love me?' Die for them!".[352] Besides, Jesus expressly said: "The good shepherd lays down his life for the sheep."[353]

Peter continues his mission as shepherd through the Pope, his successor,[354] as St. Leo the Great observes (Pope from 440 A.D. to 461 A.D.): "He has not left the helm of the Church unattended. ... And so if anything is rightly done and rightly decreed by us, if anything is won from the mercy of God by our daily supplications, it is of his work and merits whose power lives and whose authority prevails in his See."[355]

[351] St. Optatus of Milevi, *The True Church*, VII, 3.
[352] St. Augustine, *Discourse 296*, 4.
[353] Jn 10:11.
[354] Cf. *Lumen gentium*, 22; *Christus Dominus*, 2.
[355] St. Leo the Great, *Sermons*, 3, 3. The same idea is expressed in *Sermon* 4, 4.

Index of Biblical Citations

The number to the upper right indicates the footnotes where **556** biblical texts are cited.

Acts of the Apostles (Acts)

1: 1. 8[256] • 1: 3[234] • 1: 6[122-334] • 1: 8[56] • 1: 13[6-116] • 1: 14[254] • 1-15[253] • 1: 15: 26[67] • 2: 1-4[257] • 2: 5. 37-38[3] • 2: 14-36[57] • 2: 14-41[259] • 2: 22-36[274] • 2: 23. 36[60] • 2: 29[345] • 2: 32[258] • 2: 44[124-268] • 3: 1-10[65-260] • 3: 11-26[261-274] • 3: 14[60-186] • 3: 22-24[191] • 4: 1-22[263] • 4: 4[262] • 4: 5-6[264] • 4: 8-12[274] • 4: 12[2] • 4: 13[61] • 4: 13. 29. 31[345] • 4: 19-20[62] • 4: 20[252] • 4: 27. 30[186] • 4: 29[266] • 4: 31[267] • 4: 32[124] • 4: 32. 34[268] • 5: 1-11[269] • 5: 12[276] • 5: 15[66-277] • 5: 17-21[63] • 5: 17-41[272] • 5: 41[346] • 6: 2[270] • 8: 5-8. 26-40[283] • 8: 9-25[273] • 9: 3-7[64] • 9: 26[296] • 9: 26-28[292] • 9: 31[279] • 9: 32-35[65] • 9: 32-42[278] • 9: 36-42[65] • 9: 40[65] • 10: 9-16[64] • 10: 9-48[283] • 10: 34-43[274] • 10: 40[60-265] • 10: 40-41[234] • 11: 1-3. 18[284] • 11: 20-21[285] • 11: 26[286] • 11: 30[296] • 11: 34-43[58] • 12: 1-19[280] • 12: 6-11[63] • 12: 25[296] • 13: 16-41[274] • 13: 31[234] • 14: 8-18[65] • 15: 1-2[288] • 15:1-29[296] • 15:2[291-296] • 15:5[297] • 15:5-11[68] • 15:7[281-282] • 15: 7-11[298] • 15: 12[299] • 15: 22-32[303] • 16: 1. 3[306] • 16: 9[64] • 16: 25-34[63] • 18: 9-10[64] • 19: 11-12[66] • 20: 7-12[65] • 20: 22-23[64] • 21: 10-11[64] • 21: 26[307] • 22: 6-11[64] • 23: 11[64] • 26: 13-18[64] • 27: 23-24[64] • 28: 7-10[65]

1 Corinthians (1 Cor)

1: 12[69] • 3: 22[69] • 8: 13[307] • 8: 7[302] • 8: 7-13[300] • 9: 5[69] • 9: 19-21[300] • 9: 20-22[307] • 15: 5[70-237] • 15: 5-8[234]

Deuteronomy (Deut)

14: 21[301]

Exodus (Ex)
3:14[182] • 4:1-9[200] • 16:1-35[180] • 16:2:7-8[183] • 22:30[301] • 30: 11-16[100]

Ezekiel (Ezk)
6: 7. 10. 13. 14[182] • 20: 37[241] • 34[241] • 34: 23-24[241]

Galatians (Gal)
1: 18[296] • 1: 18-19[71-292] • 1: 19[280] • 2: 1[296] • 2: 1-10[296] • 2: 2[72-294] • 2: 4[289] • 2: 5[289] • 2: 7[282] • 2: 8[73-295] • 2: 9[75-293-304] • 2: 10[296] • 2: 11-14[74-305] • 5: 2[290]

Genesis (Gen)
17: 15[128] • 17: 5[127] • 32: 29[129] • 48: 15[241] • 49: 24[241]

Hosea (Hos)
4: 16[241]

Isaiah (Is)
22: 20-22[172] • 40: 11[241] • 43: 10[182] • 44: 28[241] • 63: 11[241]

Jeremiah (Jer)
10: 21[241] • 23: 1-2[241] • 50: 17-18[241]

John (Jn)
1: 34[168] • 1: 35-42[108] • 1: 41[154] • 1: 42[126] • 1: 43-51[116] • 1: 44[79] • 2: 12[91] • 3: 4[181] • 4: 10. 14[182] • 4: 15[181] • 4: 19[154] • 4: 29[154] • 4: 42[157] • 4: 54[96] • 6: 1[110] • 6: 1-13[179] • 6: 14[155] • 6: 16-21[197] • 6: 22-69[178] • 6: 30[205] • 6: 34. 48-51[182] • 6: 35. 41. 48. 51[182] • 6: 59[83] • 6: 59-66[92] • 6: 68-69[177] • 6: 69[43-333] • 7:20[160] • 7:37[182] • 7:43[159] • 8: 12[182] • 8:24. 28. 58[182] • 8:48[165] • 8:48. 52[160] • 9:5[182] • 10: 7. 9[182] • 10: 11[41-353] • 10:11.14[182-242] • 10:11.17[351] • 10:16[244] • 10:19-20[159] • 10: 20[161] • 10: 20[160] • 10: 33[166] • 11: 25[182] • 12: 25[250] •

13: 1-20[210] • 13: 6-11[35-338] • 13: 19[182] • 13: 23[48] •
13: 23-26[52-219] • 13: 25[50] • 13: 36-37[45-246] •
13: 33. 36-38[218] • 14: 6[182] • 14: 31[212] • 15: 25[182] •
16: 32[51] • 17: 18-19[185] • 18: 3[222] • 18: 10[37] •
18:10-11[38-211] • 18:15-16[49-53-226] • 18:17.25-27[13-225-342] •
18: 27[228] • 19: 26-27[46-48-49] • 20: 1-2[231] • 20: 2-4. 8[49] •
20: 2-10[54] • 20: 14. 15-19. 26[234] • 20: 28[168] •
21: 1-14[36-111] • 21: 1-23[238] • 21: 3-4[87] • 21: 4. 13[234] •
21: 7. 20. 23-24[48] • 21: 15-17[40-344] • 21: 17[230] •
21: 17-21[33] • 21: 18-22[42] • 21: 23[251] • 21: 24[47] •
21: 23[215]

Judges (Jdq)
6: 7[130] • 6: 17[201]

2 Kings (2 Kings)
17: 24-41[165] • 18: 18[172]

Leviticus (Lev)
17: 10. 12[301] • 17: 15[301] • 18: 6-18[301]

Luke (Lk)
1: 4[76] • 1: 18[202] • 1: 34-37[203] • 3: 22[193] • 4: 21[191] •
4:31-33[83] • 4:31-41[94] • 4:32[106] • 4:34[186] • 4:38-39[82-118] •
4: 42-44[104-136] • 5: 1[109] • 5: 1-11[7-25-111] • 5: 3[88] • 5: 5[87] •
5: 10[90-105] • 5: 11[117] • 5: 19[247] • 5: 21[166] • 5: 26[107] •
5: 27-28[93] • 6: 13-16[6-116] • 6: 14-16[21] • 7: 1-10[96] •
7: 34[164-167] • 8: 22-25[206] • 8: 28[168] • 8: 40-56[97] •
8: 45[140] • 8: 51[189] • 9: 7[151] • 9: 10[80] • 9: 10-17[179] •
9: 18-21[150] • 9: 20[15-168-184] • 9: 22[27] • 9: 28-36[188] •
9:32[8] • 10:46[336] • 10:13-16[99] • 10:15[78] • 12:35-48[145] •
12:39[146] • 12:41[138] • 12:42-48[139] • 15:2[167] • 17:3[132] •
17: 5-6[207] • 17: 33[250] • 17: 34[133] • 18: 18[156] •
18: 28-30[123-331] • 18: 34[174] • 21: 5-7[143] • 21: 8-33[148] •
21: 12-19[271] • 21: 16[248] • 22: 3-5[221] • 22: 8-13[209] •
22: 28[31-214] • 22: 31-32[32-215] • 22: 33[208] • 22: 42[212] •

22: 47-48[222] • 22: 50[28] • 22: 50-51[211] • 22: 54[226] •
22: 55-62[13-225-342] • 22: 60[228] • 22: 61[29-229] • 23: 2[163] •
24: 3[231] • 24: 9-10[232] • 24: 11-12[233] • 24: 15. 36[234] •
24: 19[154] • 24: 26[173] • 24: 33-34[34-236] • 24: 41-43[239] •
24: 47-48[55]

2 Maccabees (2 Mac)
2: 1-12[153] • 15: 13-16[153]

Mark (Mk)
1: 11[193] • 1: 14-20[142] • 1: 16[89-108-112] • 1: 16-18[247] •
1:16-20[7-26] • 1:17[113] • 1:18.20[117] • 1:21[83] • 1:21-34[94] •
1:22[106] • 1:24[186] • 1:29-31[82] • 1:30-31[65] • 1:35-38[104-136] •
2: 1-12[95] • 2: 6[166] • 2: 9-13-14[93] • 2: 12[107] • 2: 14[116] •
3: 16[125] • 3: 16-19[6-21-116] • 3: 17[86] • 3: 21[161] • 3: 22[160] •
4: 35-41[206] • 4: 40[275] • 5: 21-43[97] • 5: 31[140] • 5: 37[189] •
5: 41[65] • 6: 13[151] • 6: 32-44[179] • 6: 45[80] • 6: 45-52[197] •
6: 52[199] • 7: 14-23[137] • 7: 17[137] • 8: 22[81] • 8: 27-30[150] •
8:29[15-168-184] • 8:31-33[176-335] • 8:33[9] • 9:2-8[188] • 9:3[190] •
9: 6[8] • 9: 33[336] • 9: 45[174] • 10: 17[156] • 10: 28-31[123-331] •
10: 35-40[121-175-337] • 11: 21[141] • 11: 22[206] • 11: 23[207] •
13: 1-4. 32[143] • 13: 5-31[148] • 13: 9. 13[271] • 13: 33[144] •
13:34-37[145] • 14:10-11[221] • 14:26-31[213] • 14:27[30-216] •
14: 29[240] • 14: 32-38[189] • 14: 33-38[223] • 14: 36[212] •
14: 37[11-340] • 14: 44-45[222] • 14: 47[211] • 14: 50[12-275-341] •
14: 54[226] • 14: 66-72[13-225-342] • 14: 71[14-224] • 14: 72[228] •
16:5[231] • 16:6-7[235] • 16:7[232] • 16:8[232] • 16:9.12.14[234] •
16: 15[255] • 16: 15-16[55] • 22: 29. 31[208]

Matthew (Mt)
3: 17[193] • 4: 1-11[10] • 4: 13[91] • 4: 18[89-108] • 4: 18-20[247] •
4: 18-22[7-26] • 4: 19[113] • 4: 22[117] • 5: 17[192] • 5: 45[102] •
6: 12[135] • 7: 24-25[170] • 7: 28[106] • 8: 5-13[85-96] •
8: 14-15[82] • 8: 14-16[94] • 8: 23-27[206] • 8: 26[119] •
9: 1-8[95] • 9: 3[166] • 9: 8[107] • 9: 9[84-93-116] • 9: 14[20] •
9: 18-26[97] • 9: 25[189] • 9: 27[158] • 9: 27-33[98] • 9: 36[243] •

2 Peter (2 Pet)
1: 1[310] • 1: 3-11[326] • 1: 14[310] • 1: 15[310] • 1: 16-18[188-195-310] •
1: 16-21[329] • 2: 1-22[328] • 2: 16-21[329] • 3: 1[310] • 3: 3-10[330] •
3: 11-18[327]

Psalms (Ps)
44: 12. 23[241] • 74: 1[241] • 76: 21[241] • 77: 21[241] •
78: 24[180] • 78: 52-53[241] • 78: 71-72[241] • 78: 72[241] •
80: 2[241]

Romans (Rom)
14: 21[307]

2 Samuel (2 Sam)
5: 2[241]

2 Timothy (2 Tim)
3: 16[77]

Zechariah (Zech)
11: 4-5[241]

Zephaniah (Zeph)
3: 19[241]

Index

Grafiche Grilli srl
Via Manfredonia Km 2,200 - 71100 Foggia
Tel. 0881 568040 / 568034 - Fax 0881 755525
www.grafichegrilli.it · e-mail: info@grafichegrilli.it